ISBN 0-918238-01-3

Library of Congress Catalog Card Number:

76-51646

The last number on the left indicates the last printing:

7/8/9/10

# THE *Timber Framing* BOOK

## STEWART ELLIOTT
## EUGENIE WALLAS

### DRAWINGS BY LINDA FOSS

## HOUSESMITHS PRESS

P.O. BOX 157 · KITTERY POINT, MAINE 03905

*To*
*Sarah and Aaron*
*the next*
*generation*

# NOTES AND ACKNOWLEDGEMENTS

Several generations ago, a master carpenter was hired by families or communities to provide the skill, labor and tools he had inherited from his elders. It was his responsibility to perpetuate both the history and methodology of building and to teach those who would carry on after him. Unfortunately, this kind of self-help from one generation to the next is not in practice today. Consequently, as the old-timers pass on, there is no one to perpetuate the tradition or the methods of timber framing. We have written this book, therefore, as a "how was" as well as a "how to" book. We hope it can serve some of the functions that the master carpenter fulfilled.

We would like to thank the many interested people who have asked questions about building timber frames. These people include our suppliers who support our unusual building methods and philosophies. Their interest and willingness to help have contributed to our success as a business. The backbone of the business is our dedicated group of craftsmen and women, and our architectural designer. Their varied skills enable Housesmiths to explore our building heritage and to apply this knowledge to the constantly changing needs of today. We want to thank them as well.

The book could not have been written without the help of many energetic people who have reacted positively with their comments, and who have given many hours of dedicated work. Don Goodwin, Silas and Constance Weeks, and Roth Wilkofsky were among the initial supporters of the book. Mary-Catherine Deibel has spent many long and late hours editing several drafts for the book. It is difficult to write about a craft in a way that makes the information useable to the reader. With her expertise, Mary-Catherine has made timber framing a comprehensible subject.

Alexandra and Page Mead have worked closely with us on the book. Alexandra has spent long hours typing and revising several drafts, offering valuable consultation on text and layout. Page has been the overall coordinator for the book. He has arranged meetings, set up distribution schedules and locations, scheduled the many phases of the process, and conducted research for the book. He has spent many hours consulting with various people about the publishing aspects. We decided early in the process that we wanted to write, print, bind and distribute the book ourselves. We thank Page and Alexandra for making this possible.

The thanking of a co-author is a difficult thing to do. Genie waded through mountains of illegible handwritten notes about a subject that was then foreign to her, putting philosophies and ideas in their proper perspective. And because she knows me and the buildings inside and out, she could put into words all of my mental gymnastics. Genie is the co-author in the truest sense. Her limitless energy and unending support provided the impetus for the creation and completion of every phase of *The Timber Framing Book*. A very special thanks to Genie.

*STEWART ELLIOTT*

# CONTENTS

# INTRODUCTION

It was July 4, 1975, a fine Maine day for the Fourth and an even better day for a barn raising. Stacy Wentworth had taken down an old barn that had stood on family land near the ocean in Kennebunk. He had saved the timbers and they were being used to frame the Wentworths' new barn.

Stacy and Marilyn had invited their friends for the raising, and on that day more than 100 of them — men, women and kids — arrived to raise the Wentworths' barn. Only Stewart Elliott among them had ever raised a timber frame before, but that didn't lessen anyone's enthusiasm for the job. There was plenty of work to be done, and hard work it was, but everyone pitched in and the job got done.

There was also swimming in the pond, laughter and a potluck feast that would have been the envy of any baronial dining hall. But most impressive of all was the feeling everyone had that they were part of a real community. Strangers worked together, sweated together, joked together and became friends.

The raising took a little longer than had been expected, but by Sunday night the last rafter was raised, the ridge pole was in place and Stacy had climbed aloft to nail the traditional pine bough in place at the peak. The Wentworths had a barn frame and their friends had experienced a Fourth of July they'll never forget.

It seems to me that the sense of community, the idea of bending one's back to help one's neighbor, is the essence of timber framing. You can't raise a frame by yourself. It takes people, a lot of people if the frame to be raised is a large one, and when people work hard together doing something as worthwhile as helping a friend raise a house or barn, they can't help feeling good about it and about themselves.

A raising is a celebration. When the Housesmiths raise a frame, they nail the pine bough to the peak, tap a keg of beer and have a party. Once they even hired a one-man band to play for the occasion. I've never heard of that happening in Levittown, or anywhere else that rows and rows of conventional stud wall houses are being built.

Timber framing offers many alternatives, but I believe the most important of them is the alternative to conventional, mass-produced, anonymously built houses that it offers. I suppose the economics of timber framing can be argued, particularly if you live in a part of the country where massive timbers aren't readily available. But what can't be argued is that feeling of having accomplished something good, of having built something good and lasting, of having shared in an important task, that comes to people raising a timber frame. That's what timber framing is all about, and timber framing is what this book is all about. Enjoy it, enjoy your timber-frame house, and enjoy yourselves.

Jim Martin

Eliot, Maine

March, 1977

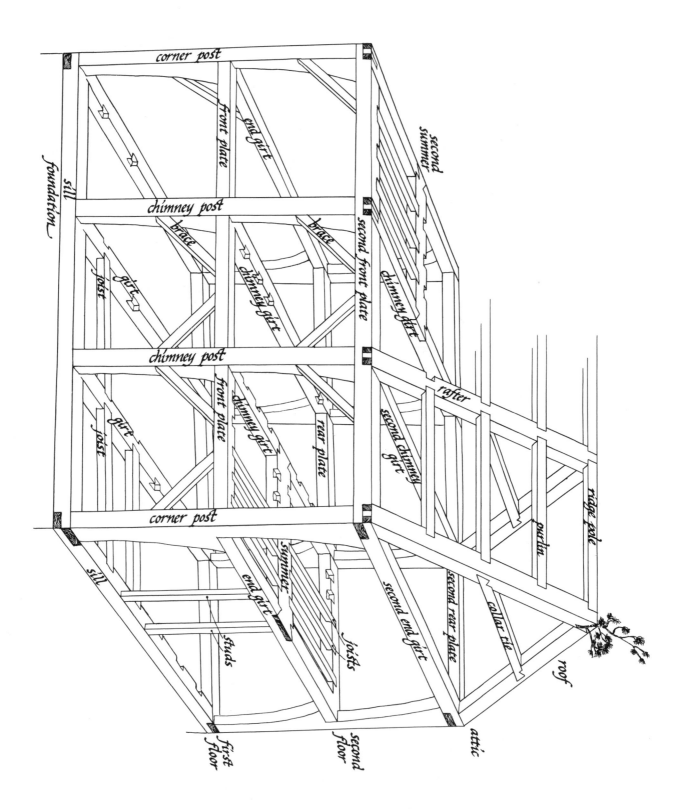

# FOREWORD

This book is being written for those of you who want to learn how to build a timber-frame house. For the past several years, we've been building such houses for folks in New England because we think that they provide both beautiful and durable shelter for people. We have discovered that an increasing number of our clients are interested in participating in the design and construction of the houses they will be spending part of their lives in. In sympathy with that interest, we find ourselves trying to describe the principles of timber framing over the phone, or scribbling house plans and joint diagrams on matchbook covers or doughnut box-tops. We began to realize that there is now a need for an organized source of information on the planning and building of a timber-frame structure.

Early craftsmen abandoned timber framing as smaller sawn, standard lumber and inexpensive nails became available. Today, however, many sizes and lengths of timbers are available from lumber mills (who will deliver your order to your building site), and nails are no longer inexpensive. Therefore, we have returned to timber framing and we would like to share with you several of the considerations which persuaded us to adopt and recommend this method of construction.

We have discovered that there are structural, economic and aesthetic advantages to timber framing. A timber-frame house offers more strength than a conventionally framed house because the frame bears the weight, as in the human skeleton; the walls (like skin) mainly provide closure. Since the timber frame is jointed together, it needs few nails or bolts which weather more quickly than wood pegs. Because windows can be mounted on the frame, rather than on the sheathing, the system is strong and weather-tight. History provides the best test for durability. Timber-frame houses built in Europe as early as the fourteenth century stand, proud and sturdy, to this day.

Compared to conventional construction, timber-frame structures can be 20 to 30 percent less expensive to build. Less energy is expended in both the milling and the construction of the frame. Although it takes just as long to mill a 2" x 4" as it does a major timber, there are far fewer timbers in a timber structure than there are 2" x 4"s in a conventional frame. The fact that we use native lumber considerably reduces transportation costs and the amount of time and energy we expend on the job. For people interested in using wood heat, timbers absorb and retain heat more efficiently than a conventionally framed house. The sun's warming of the solid mass of wood in a timber frame works to the advantage of a solar heating system as well.

The timber-frame house is, by the standards both of nature and of tradition, beautiful. The exposed framing in a finished timber house is one of its most attractive features; structural and finish work merge and become one phase of construction. A timber-frame house owner has a wide range of choice as to what kinds of walls and ceilings he wants. The acoustics of a timber-frame house are better than those of a conventional structure, since the diversity of surfaces in the exposed frame reduces echoes. You will discover that in timber-frame structures, there are no large surfaces that force light to reflect harshly; natural and lamp light diffuse softly and warmly, enhanced by the wood. The basic plan of a timber-frame house adapts well to various arrangements of interior space and to any future additions the owner might decide to build, since there is no structural necessity for partitions. Rooms can be large and open. You can fill your rooms with hanging pots and pans, plants, tools, or hammocks, since the frame itself is a natural and happy place from which to suspend anything.

If you have some basic carpentry skills, you and some helpers can frame a house using the information in this book. If you do not, and have a carpenter in mind who has not previously used timber framing, he can use this book to teach himself how.

What we are presenting here is our preference for timber framing as it was used by the early settlers in the New England colonies. We admire the traditional and functional qualities of such framing; it is aesthetically pleasing and allows for flexibility in design. Perhaps most important to us is the fact that the method was conceived by men who relied on only their own manpower to build their houses; timber framing does not require any extraordinary equipment, or even electrical power. The methodology is simple and honest and utilitarian, with form following function.

We invite you to return, as we have, to New England-style timber framing. We think you'll find the process of raising your own timber-frame house an extremely satisfying experience.

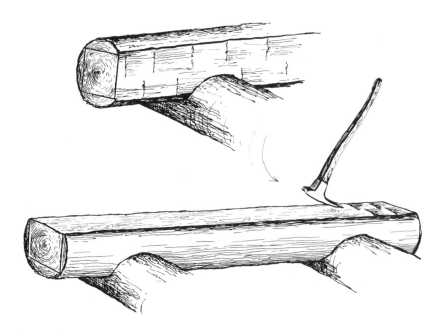

# 1 HISTORICAL BACKGROUND

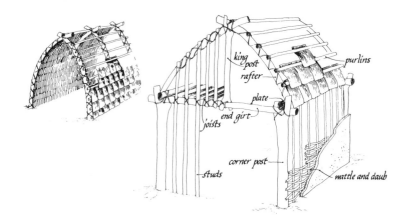

The history of timber framing is very much a part of our rationale for building timber-frame houses. Therefore, we will begin our book by giving you a brief outline of that history.

Timber framing is a tradition and a skill that has its roots in the Egyptian cultures of 2,000 B.C. No one knows who came along first, the carpenter or the furniture maker. We do know that furniture making and timber framing use the same system of joinery. Farmers were traditionally their own carpenters and furniture makers. Using the same system of joinery for both tasks simplified their life.

When the first settlers arrived in America, they were faced with a variety of obstacles, the most urgent of which was housing. There were no local housing models to copy. What the settlers knew about English architecture didn't help much to acclimate them to their new environment, with its extremes in temperature and its periods of rain and drought. Their first homes were very primitive. They scraped out a dugout under a hillside, and made a fire against the wall on the highest side, but they soon found that smoke and heavy rains made their sod huts uninhabitable.

The colonists were forced to develop their own method of building, taking into consideration factors such as climate, available materials, and the capacities of their own labor force.

Wood, stone, marble, slate, sand and clay were abundant in New England, but masons, carpenters, sawyers and tools were not. When skilled craftsmen and tools began to arrive from Europe, the settlers started to duplicate the methods of construction prevalent in England and Holland at that time. They used the wattle and daub method, that is, a wood frame was filled in with woven twigs and smeared with mud. Later, when bricks became available, the spaces in the frame were filled in with brick nogging.

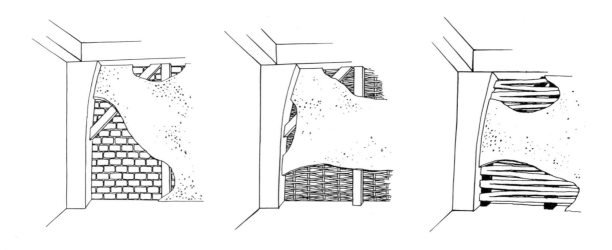

In England, the settlers had already learned about the properties of white oak in their construction. They continued to make use of this wood in both frame and finish work in spite of the abundance of more easily workable hard and soft woods in America. This tradition survived in the colonies until as late as 1800, when the abundant, native pine came into use.

The settlers were eventually forced to modify the wattle and daub method. They were discovering that extremes of weather made the wood frames and nogging shrink and swell and eventually crack. Soon, nogging was eliminated altogether, as the colonists found that clapboard exteriors and plaster interiors provided more protective walls. At this point, in the early 1600s, the log cabin was virtually unheard of as yet in New England, and one structure the colonists had experimented with, a stockade of sharpened logs driven into the ground and filled in with mud, had proven impractical. Therefore, the New Englanders directed their energies toward perfecting and expanding the wood-frame, clapboard-sheathed cottage. It was their solution to the problem of shelter in their new environment.

These houses set the standard both for strength and for security against climatic and environmental menaces. The timbers were squared with a broad axe and finished with an adze. Planks and boards were cut with a pit saw. It was an arduous task for two men; one worked from above and one from below, using a long, straight saw. Even though it took only 13 years from the time the first settlers arrived to establish the first water power saw at the Falls of the Great Works River in Maine, labor was at a premium.

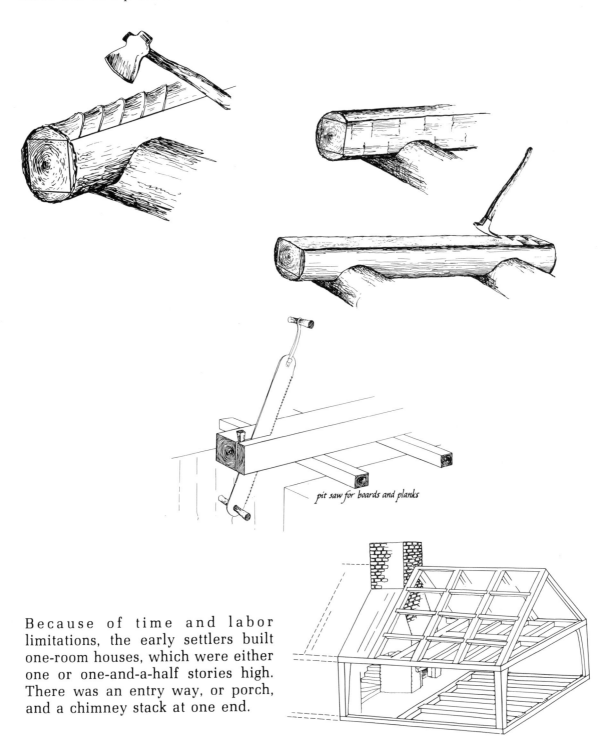

*pit saw for boards and planks*

Because of time and labor limitations, the early settlers built one-room houses, which were either one or one-and-a-half stories high. There was an entry way, or porch, and a chimney stack at one end.

By 1675, modifications of this plan developed. A second room was added on the other side of the chimney, creating space for a kitchen and a living room. The house now had a central source of heat. Then, by raising the roof and adding a "lean-to" along the back length of the house, a second story was created. The design, known as the saltbox design, allowed for three rooms on the first floor and an attic on the second. By 1700, householders were using the saltbox design as a plan, rather than just as a means of expansion, for their cottages. Very soon, the lean-to was abandoned in favor of the full two story house, in which the second floor attic was replaced by three rooms. We mentioned before that we consider the inherent flexibility for adding rooms and stories to be one of the important advantages of timber framing (one that the early settlers counted on). Even though few of us begin building with just one room today, the evolution of design in timber framing illustrates the many options we have for structural expansion as our space needs change.

Hand-hewn timbers jointed together and secured with pegs remained the method of construction until the early decades of the nineteenth century. In the 1830s, as inexpensive machine-made nails and standardized sawn lumber became available, the balloon frame house came into being. The lighter frame and simplified labor requirements of balloon framing appeared at a time when both transportation and milling techniques were still primitive. The timber-frame method was soon replaced by the new, faster and more economical process. By this time, however, the colonists had successfully adapted their housing to their new-world environment. Their structures were compact, low-ceilinged, centrally heated by a large fireplace, protected by small windows covered with oilcloth, weather-tightened by clapboards, and secured with roofs with pitches that could shed the rains and snows of New England.

We will be talking about methods for building a timber frame, methods very much like the ones of the 1750s. Our frames reflect the traditional proportions, ceiling heights, roof pitches and structural systems which the colonists developed in response to their needs. We have the advantage of choosing to follow in their tradition not because we need to, but because we have found their methods practical and the finished product beautiful.

But before we do that, let's examine the specific reasons that we, as modern builders, prefer timber-frame structures.

# 2 WHY TIMBER FRAMING?

Timber framing is a personal statement made by the builder-owner. From the beginning, the work is both a process and product, to be seen and enjoyed, to take pride in and to use. This involvement between builder and building sets timber framing apart from other methods of modern construction. A timber frame is a handcrafted piece of work fashioned from the best of materials — wood. The end product is a living, breathing, organic structure which will last many generations. The high quality of workmanship in the frame, its strength, durability, and beauty, can serve as a model for all the many generations of people who will live in and look at the house.

Timber framing seems to have many limitations. For example, a timber frame must be built by hand if it is to be properly done. It demands that the builder use care, traditional tools, a lot of time, and have an understanding of tradition. The timbers are heavy, and it takes many hands to raise them. The frame is also limited in size (there will never be a timber-frame skyscraper) and style (the system of timber framing tends to dictate a box or rectangular shaped house). The massive roof system is an expensive one, and therefore the pitch should be steep so that there is as much space as possible under the roof; the basic cape, saltbox, garrison, gambrel and two story styles of timber-frame homes evolved from this inherent roof/space limitation. It takes more man hours to complete a timber frame than a conventional 2'' x 4'' frame. The method also requires more equipment and special tools — tools which are traditional and might require time to acquire and master.

But the uniqueness of the timber frame derives from the fact that its seeming limitations turn out to be its assets. The frame that takes more time and more people to raise is the frame that becomes an act of friendship, a community effort. Timber framing provides the situation in which people can help one another, in which people make a commitment to each other and to their homes. We feel that traditional methods and tools and building by hand help us to appreciate the better, more substantial kind of life that we are trying to reintroduce into our communities. The age-old styles of timber-frame houses also fit the spirit and climate of New England. These new homes will depend on the use of local resources, labor and materials. In contrast to timber framing, automated construction seems to us to be thoroughly unacceptable. The timber-frame home will still be standing when the "little boxes on the hillside" fall down; they will prove to be an asset rather than a liability to a town.

We look to the craftsman to produce such high quality work. Who is he? He does not need to have accrued thirty years of experience or to have come from a family of craftsmen to produce fine work. However, expertise is acquired with experience and time. A craftsman is anyone who wants and needs to lavish care on his work. This sense of dedication pervades his methods and dominates the philosophy and tradition from which the craft has emerged. The owner-builder of a timber-frame house can be this craftsman. He can learn and even become quite proficient at the skills, though it will be a challenge, and will take some practice. Craftsmanship has always been an important factor in timber framing. The materials and methods demand individual concentration as well as a carefully coordinated group effort among the owner-builder and his carpenter/helpers. A home built with this kind of care will be meaningful not only to the family that lives in the house but also to the community that has participated in its construction.

To become a good craftsman, one must first learn the rules of good workmanship.

## FIRST, THINK ABOUT THE PROJECT IN ITS ENTIRETY

What is the nature of the job? Is it going to be visible, and if so, how much of it and by whom will it be seen? Does the end product have to work — can it resist people, support a horse, or rain or snow? Will it be portable, stationary, permanent, or temporary, and to what degree? How long does it have to last — hours, days, weeks, months or years? Is the task part of a whole or an end in itself?

What are the tools necessary for the job?

What are the materials necessary for the job?

How are you going to transport your tools, equipment, and materials to the job?

What is the follow-through and the clean up process?

## SECOND, ASK YOURSELF IF YOU ARE CAPABLE OF DOING THE JOB

Ask this only after you have considered all of the factors above.

Proceed if you can.

If you cannot, admit it, and ask, read, observe and practice until you can. You can ask Housesmiths for help on any phase of the planning or building of your house.

## THIRD, PREPARE FOR THE JOB

Think of the logical order in which the job should be done.

Organize all the tools and materials before you start to transport them to the site.

Have the materials and tools on hand and make sure there is enough of everything.

Set up the necessary equipment, staging, and temporary jigs you will need for the job.

Organize all materials by the order of their use and their size.

Choose a place for waste so that clean-up will not be a major undertaking.

Devote all your initial energy to making sure you have everything you need when you get to the job.

## FOURTH, THE EXECUTION OF THE JOB

Learn the logical order of completing every part of every job.

### Preparation

Find all the materials, tools, equipment, and measurements you'll need.

### Assembly

Put each piece together as preparation for the next piece, with each step achieving a higher degree of finish. The amount of skill you display and the amount of time you spend should be appropriate to the stage of construction. In other words, rough work demands rough materials and rough skills; finish work demands good materials and a high degree of skill. Know where you can fudge — what will be seen in the end product.

### Completion and Follow-Through

A job is complete when all the component parts have been assembled successfully and the work has been accepted by whoever is responsible for the job. A successful job is one in which the materials and workmanship serve the purpose for which they were designed for the duration of the time the product is expected to last.

### Clean-up

A job has a specific time and place. When it is complete, all items no longer related to it must be removed. Return and store all tools, equipment and materials so they are ready for the next job.

A mechanic can obey all these rules. But what makes a craftsman? A professional craftsman executes a job in an efficient, economical and perceptive way, deciding as he goes along how best to use his skill and his time. He is able to arrange his work so that there is always a built-in cushion to account for all irregularities and human inaccuracy; at the same time he makes sure that he is producing a beautiful, structurally sound product. He knows how to hide the ragged corners. He understands the future of the job and the materials, how they will react to weather, loads and forces. He knows which measurements are the critical ones. He knows where the greatest chances of error are, and how to reduce those chances. He is always checking his work and his measurements by using an alternate method of calculating. He has a constant visual image of the end product. He knows that measuring with a ruler of any sort is only a method of transporting the relative size of something from one place to another. He recognizes that this is one of the easiest ways to make a mistake, either because one can read the rule incorrectly or not accurately enough. He adds again, subtracts again, and tests his memory.

The craftsman's way of avoiding mistakes is to measure as little as possible. When he does measure, he does so two or three times, and cuts only once. He scribes as much of his work as he can by holding one piece in place and marking it to the existing situation. Or he makes a template for repetitive work. He understands his tools, their capabilities, their limitations, their design and function. He knows that levels and squares are also always relative and only represent the actual situation. He knows that measuring tools can be interpreted in various ways, and each is affected daily by location and weather. He knows his tools and his skill allows him to adjust to their eccentricities.

In the heart of any good craftsman is a good attitude. He must care about his project, his tools, the tradition and philosophy of his craft, and the durability and beauty of his creation. Anyone who seriously undertakes the task of building himself a timber frame, of learning the methods, and acquiring the tools, steadfastly lifting and cutting, fitting and adjusting, deserves on raising day to call himself a craftsman.

# 3 GETTING STARTED

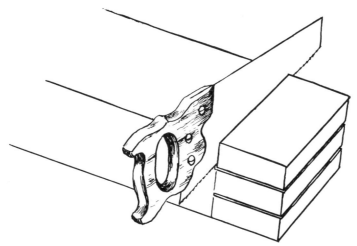

Now that you know some of the history of the traditional, timber-frame house, let us say that there were as many variations on the basic design as there were prototypes of it. There was no one way that any of the framing was always done. For example, summer timbers can run from the front of the house to the back, or from side to side, or be excluded from the frame altogether. We have not been restricted by the notion of reproducing "*the* colonial frame." We hope that you will choose to build the frame that is most appealing to you, drawing on the traditional framing system in order to make it happen.

There are some important decisions you will be making as you design your house and before you can order your timbers.

### What size is your house going to be?

Most folks have difficulty visualizing the size of a finished house by trying to imagine its dimensions or by looking at a scale drawing. Our experience has been that the house seems, to its owner, to get bigger and bigger as it is being built. The initial staking for the excavation and foundation often looks very small. As the first floor framing and deck go down, the project begins to appear bigger. On raising day, the house is suddenly larger than life. So that you won't be spending more time and money than is necessary to produce a house that is bigger than you envisioned, we suggest that you find a cape or garrison, or any design, that you think meets your approximate space requirements, and measure it carefully. An extra 2 feet in a small cape could add as much as 1,200 dollars to your budget. The choices for interior space divisions are almost infinite, so be concerned at this point only with the overall dimensions of the house.

### Are you going to build your house alone?

It takes strong muscles to move timbers and to cut joints. If you have no power available, squaring the ends of large timbers with a one-man saw is hard, time-consuming work. If you are going to have power at your house eventually, contact your electric company about getting temporary power at your site.

The amount of time you are going to spend building is another important consideration. It takes one of us 60 hours to precut all the timbers for a 26' x 32' cape. It takes a sunny Saturday and six to ten strong friends for us to raise this entire frame, including the rafters. We have had, however, plenty of experience. You should plan on spending more time than this, and be sure to arrange for enough help.

### Where are you getting your timbers and decking?

We suggest you check with several mills, if possible, in your area to find out if the sizes of timbers you'll need are available and to find the best-priced, good quality wood. Be sure the mill can provide you with the milling you need for your materials, and that they will deliver. We use green pine for the timbers. We would like to be able to use seasoned timbers but it takes one year for 1 inch of lumber to dry and we can't wait eight years for an 8 inch timber to dry. The next best alternative is to use wintercut trees that have cured as long as possible. We use 1 or 2 inch tongue and groove pine, spruce or hemlock planed on one side for the decking.

### What tools will you need?

Although early colonists had only hand tools to work with, we suggest that you save time and effort by using power tools for at least some phases of construction. For the most part, we use power tools on parts of the frame that will not be exposed in the finished house. We use hand tools for planing, adzing, and finishing the parts that will show. (There is a glossary including tools at the end of the book.)

### What are the safety considerations?

The size and number of timbers in your frame make safety rules particularly important. You should have your foundation backfilled before you start carrying timbers around so that you will not be spanning open spaces carrying heavy wood. Be sure your tools are sharpened and in good repair; they should be checked daily.

Now you are ready to learn about the frame and its timbers.

# 4  THE FRAME

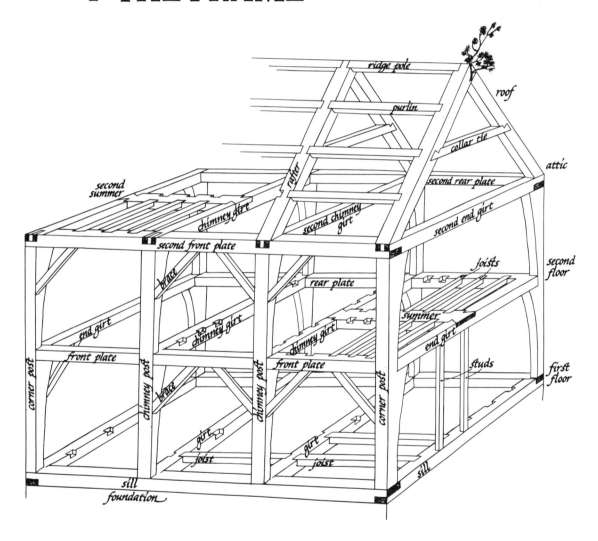

We define "frame" as the basic skeletal structure of the house. The frame consists of different sizes of timbers. The definitions of these different timbers will make a lot more sense if, as you read about them, you refer to the labeled drawing at the beginning of the book. A better way to understand a frame and its component parts is to sit in the middle of a friend's timber-frame house or barn and study the visible framing. The functions and relationships of all the parts as they form a whole will become more obvious as you begin to develop a working knowledge of timber framing.

Beginning at the foundation, the frame consists of the following timbers.

*SILLS* These are the major horizontal timbers which lie on the foundation and form the lowest part of the frame.

*POSTS* Known also as uprights, posts are erected perpendicular to the sills at specified intervals. They are also used as supports within the frame, as around masonry.

*GUNSTOCK POSTS* These are special posts which provide additional support at the points where other major timbers meet. Gunstock posts widen in size in one traverse direction from floor to ceiling.

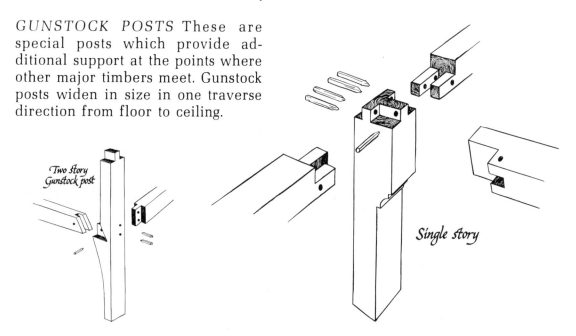

*GIRTS* These are major second or third story horizontal timbers which run from the front to the back of a structure.

*JOISTS* These are any of the smaller horizontal timbers which run parallel to each other between major timbers to fill out the structure and provide support for decks.

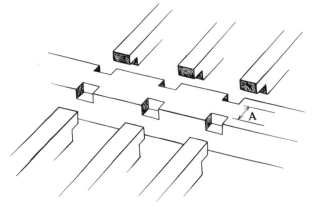

*PLATES* These are the major second or third story horizontal timbers which run from one end of the frame to the other. The plates support the rafters.

*SUMMER* This is the largest major horizontal timber spanning the girts. It runs parallel to the plates and parallel to the front of the structure. This timber can range in width from 12 to 17½ inches.

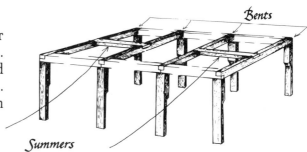

*RAFTERS* These are the sloping main timbers of the roof frame.

*PURLINS* These are horizontal members of the roof frame which run between rafters.

*RIDGE POLE* This is a horizontal timber which connects the rafters at the peak.

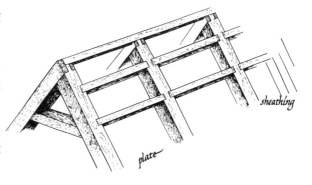

*COLLAR TIES* Running parallel to the girts, these timbers connect rafter pairs at a given height.

*BRACES* These smaller timbers are placed diagonally between posts and girts or plates to make a structure more rigid.

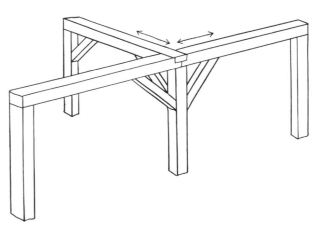

*BENT* This is a section of a frame which is composed of a line of vertical posts and the horizontal timbers that connect them.

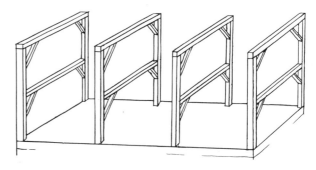

As you continue reading and begin to plan your own house, you will learn the whys and wherefores of some of the optional framing members, such as summers, collar ties, and even ridge poles. The remaining members are considered standard and only differ in their dimensions and relationships to each other in the whole.

Now that you have an overview of what the structural frame of your house consists of and looks like, we'd like to discuss the calculations and measurements that will enable you to figure out how to put it all together.

# 5 FRAMING CALCULATIONS AND MEASUREMENTS

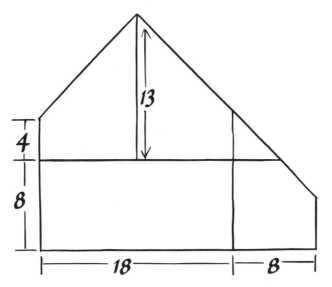

To be able to order framing materials, and to estimate both costs and time, you will need to know how to make some basic calculations and measurements. Your calculations will save you time in the long run. Figure everything on paper, order correctly, and then put all your energy into carrying out the prescribed operations. We have developed some formulas which we will present at the end of this chapter, along with our calculations for several sample situations.

First of all, before you can order materials, you will need to figure the measurements of:

> the perimeter of the building;
> the roof — the span, rise, run and pitch;
> the rafter length;
> the square footage measurements.

*PERIMETER* This is a term which describes the number of feet around your house. To find the perimeter of a square building, multiply the length of one side by four. For a rectangular building, add the width and length together and multiply by two. Finding the perimeter is necessary for determining orders for foundation materials, and for figuring measurements for sills, plates and girts.

*ROOF PITCH* and *SLOPES* These are terms which refer to the relationship of the angle of the roof to the horizontal plane of your house. The roof's function is to protect. It is sloped so that it sheds water. Our intention is always to design and build a roof that is attractive as well as effective. The proportions of the roof slopes are an important element of the tradition we respect in our building of timber-frame structures. Following tradition's example, then, we look at pitch as a relationship of the height of the ridge above the plate to the width of the building. The height of the ridge above the plate is called the *rise*, (a), and the width of the building is called the *span*, (2b). The *run*, (b), is half the span.

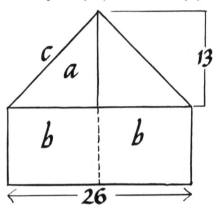

For example, 1/3 pitch means that the rise is 1/3 the width of the building. Thus, if the building is 30 feet wide, the rise is 10 feet. Sometimes the pitch is expressed as the relationship of the rafter length to the width of the building. For example, a 2/3 pitch means that the length of the rafter is 2/3 the width of the building. If the building is 27 feet wide, the rafter would be 18 feet long. In Gothic roofs, the length of the rafter is equal to the width of the building. In square pitch roofs, the rise is equal to the run and the rafters meet at right angles at the peak. Conventional builders use set formulas and tables to determine the pitch of the roof. These formulas serve only to relate the rise to the run without specifically relating the pitch to the overall building dimensions. Thus, an 8/12 pitch means that for every 12 inches that you measure in on the horizontal girt, you will measure up 8 inches on the rise.

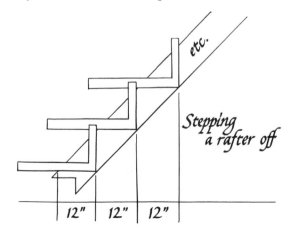

How, then, do you determine what pitch you would like? Either find an old building that has pleasing proportions and make some measurements of house width, and of rafter length and/or rise, or draw your house dimensions and design a roof that you will like. We prefer square pitches on capes, saltboxes and some barns. We have used a 1/3 pitch on two story center-chimney colonials.

*RAFTER LENGTHS* These are determined by a formula once you know the width of the building and the rise. A simple application of the $a^2 + b^2 = c^2$ formula used to determine the sides of a triangle will give you your rafter length. This is fully explained in Chapter 9.

*SQUARE FOOTAGE MEASUREMENTS* These are area measurements necessary for determining how much living area the house will have, and for ordering materials you'll need to build the frame and deck. Following are the square footage measurements you will be computing.

*USEABLE SQUARE FOOTAGE OF A BUILDING* For a square building multiply the length of one side by itself. For a two story building, multiply the downstairs area by 2.65. If it's a cape, multiply the downstairs area by 1.75 for the total useable area, and for a saltbox, multiply the downstairs area by 1.95. These are the formulas we devised so that the additional area of the attics created by traditional roof pitches is provided for. (These computations are useful only for estimating the living area of the building.)

*SQUARE FOOTAGE OF FLOORS* This area equals the length times the width times the number of stories or floors in your house, including the attic if there is to be one.

*BOARD FOOT* This is an abstract volume of lumber 1 inch thick, 12 inches wide and 12 inches long. To find out how many board feet there are in a given length or lengths of lumber, you use the following formula:

$$\frac{\text{thickness (in inches) x width (in inches) x length in feet}}{12}$$

Thus, a 3" x 5" timber 12 feet long would have:

$$\frac{3'' \times 5'' \times 12'}{12} = 15 \text{ board feet (bf).}$$

If there were 40 3" x 5"s 12 feet long, there would be:

$$\frac{40 \ (3'' \times 5'' \times 12')}{12} = 600 \text{ bf.}$$

*LINEAR FOOT* This is a term that refers to the length of any given piece of lumber. For example, 12 linear feet of 2" x 4"s is enough to cover 12 running feet.

When your frame calls for a number of pieces that are all the same length (for example, the joists), you can order them by the piece. For example, you might ask for 40 3'' x 5''s 8 feet long. This would be an alternative to figuring out the board feet in your order. The total number of board feet in your frame is a useful number for determining what your materials will cost, since lumber is frequently priced by the board foot. It's then simply a matter of multiplying the gross number of board feet of lumber in your frame by that price in order to make a fairly accurate estimate of what your frame materials will cost.

There are some useful terms associated with ordering decking. We use tongue and groove (also called matched) boards for decks. These can be planed on one side (the side you walk on) and rough on the other (the side that would be the visible ceiling of the first floor), or they can be planed on both sides for a smooth ceiling. This is called either D1S (dressed-one-side), or S1S (smooth-one-side), or, in the case of two smooth sides, D2S or S2S. You can use boards which have square smooth edges, but you will find that tongue and groove boards are stronger.

Now that we have presented the basic formulas and terminology, we will give you an example of how these calculations can actually work for you as you plan your house. We'll also give you some more of the formulas we've worked out over the years. They should provide you with some shortcuts in your figuring. First of all, let's say you're building a 26' x 32' cape. (These figures are very familiar to us since those are the dimensions of our own cape, which we built in the spring of 1975). Our roof has a square pitch and we chose 7'6'' ceilings to have room for our Shaker hutch which is 6'8''. Therefore the height to the girts is 6'9''.

First, calculate the number of square feet of useable space in the house, downstairs and upstairs. Because of its roof pitch, a cape only has three-fourths of the useable space upstairs that it has downstairs. Thus, we use the length times the width times a factor of 1.75 whenever we want to calculate the useable living space of a cape.

*USEABLE SQUARE FOOTAGE OF HOUSE:*
        downstairs = 26' x 32' = 832 sq. ft.
        upstairs = .75 x 832 sq. ft. = 624 sq. ft.
        total = 1456 sq. ft.
        *Shortcut:* (26' x 32' x 1.75 = 1456 sq. ft.)

*PERIMETER OF HOUSE:* (26' + 32') x 2 = 116'

*RAFTER LENGTH:* $a^2 + b^2 = c^2$
        $13^2 + 13^2 = c^2$
        $338 = c^2$
        18' 3 15/16'' = c or 18'4''
        *Round the figures off to the next highest foot for ordering purposes.*

The following formulas, ones we have derived, will serve as a rough guide for calculating the amount of materials you will need, and the hours you will spend to complete the framing phase of construction. These figures are only estimates, but they are very helpful for ballpark figuring.

> *FRAME* To determine the number of board feet in a frame with 1 inch thick decks, multiply the useable square footage by a factor of 4.25.

> > A 26' x 32' cape would have 1456 sq. ft. x 4.25 = 6188 bd. ft.
> >
> > A 26' x 34' saltbox would have 1723 sq. ft. x 4.25 = 7322 bd. ft.

To determine how long it will take a skilled person to cut and raise the frame, multiply the useable square footage by a factor of .15 hours.

> > A 26' x 32' cape would take 1456 sq. ft. x .15 = 218.4 hours; that is, it would take three workers 1.8 weeks, or it would take one man 5.4 weeks.
> >
> > A 26' x 34' saltbox would take 1723 sq. ft. x .15 = 258.5 hrs.

*DECKS* To roughly determine the number of board feet of lumber in a 2 inch thick deck, multiply the useable square footage by a factor of 2.70.

> > The cape would have 1456 sq. ft. x 2.70 = 3931 bd. ft.
> >
> > The saltbox would have 1723 sq. ft. x 2.70 = 4652 bd. ft.

To determine how long it will take you to lay the deck, multiply useable square footage times a factor of .03 hours.

> > The cape decks would take 1456 sq. ft. x .03 = 43.68 hrs.
> >
> > The saltbox would take 1723 sq. ft. x .03 = 51.69 hrs.

If you're laying a 1 inch subfloor and a 1 inch finish floor, your time estimate for laying the decks will be determined by multiplying useable square footage by a factor of .02 for the subfloor and a factor of .1 for the finish floor, which requires more care and time.

For the cape: 1456 sq. ft. x .02 = 29 hrs.

> 1456 sq. ft. x .1 = 145.6 hrs.

> And for the saltbox: 1723 sq. ft. x .02 = 3.46 hrs.

> 1723 sq. ft. x .1 = 172.3 hrs.

If you use tile in the bath and/or the kitchen, there will be fewer board feet to order, and there will be fewer board feet to lay, thereby diminishing the time factor. You can either lay a deck once using 2 inch stock, or lay it twice using a 1 inch subfloor covered with a 1 inch finish floor. The advantage to the method of laying a 2 inch deck once is that it is practical and saves time. It's finished at once — you will not need to move heavy appliances and furniture around later when it's time to finish the floor. However, if your initial capital is limited and you are interested in taking advantage of an opportunity to save money, you can defer half your flooring expense till later by laying just the 1 inch subfloor. For example, in the 26' x 32' cape, the materials alone would cost 320 dollars more (at our local prices) for 2 inch decking than for 1 inch decking.

*TIME TO COMPLETE THE ENTIRE HOUSE* This can vary to a large extent, depending on your foundation, the masonry, and the degree of finish detail, but you can roughly estimate the time the whole project will take by multiplying square footage times a factor of .01 weeks. This formula is based on a work force of six people.

> For a cape, 1456 sq. ft. x .01 weeks equals 14.6 weeks for six people.
> For a saltbox, 1723 sq. ft. x .01 weeks equals 17.2 weeks for six people.

You should by now have made some basic decisions about your house: how big your house will be, how high the ceilings will be, what pitch the roof will be, and so on. These decisions, translated into figures, will allow you to communicate with your suppliers. Before we take a look at how to devise your own particular frame, we think it might be important to take a look at how all these pieces of the frame get put together, that is, how joinery works. We've chosen to discuss joinery at this point because we want you to know what is involved in cutting your joints before you decide how many sticks you will need, and before you decide what sticks will be included in your particular frame. If time and labor are restricted, you may choose to use simpler joinery and fewer, larger timbers. If you are working as a community with lots of time for the project, perhaps you will choose to go full tilt in terms of the joinery. The flexibility of the New England timber-frame tradition allows you to do either and still be true to its heritage. The builders of two hundred years ago had the same problems you will face.

# 6 JOINERY

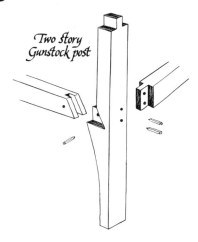

*Two Story Gunstock post*

## DEFINITIONS

Joinery is the craft of connecting and securing the separate members of the frame to one another by means of specific cuts on the ends and/or sides of the timbers. Each of these joints has a name and is usually some variation of a hole or slot on one timber, and a corresponding, matching projection on the other. Following are definitions and drawings of the joints you will most likely use.

*SIMPLE MORTISE AND TENON* A mortise is a hole or slot in a timber, and is also called a pocket, housing, or the female part of the joint. A tenon, called the male portion of the joint, is the projection which fits into the mortise. The tenon can either be a) a *central tenon* or b) a *full-width tenon*. A third type of mortise and tenon is the *tusk joint* where the tenon goes all the way through the corresponding mortise. This joint is used at the point where posts are joined to sills, girts and plates.

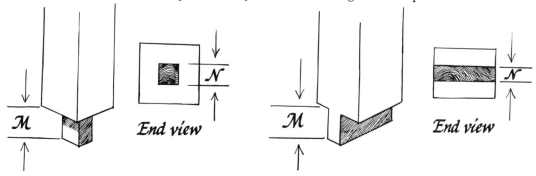

*HALF-LAP* In this joint, the mortise is an L-shaped notch on one timber and the tenon a corresponding L-shaped projection. A half-lap joint can also describe a situation in which each timber being joined has an identical and corresponding L-shaped portion removed from its ends. The half-lap is used where joists join the sills, plates, girts and/or summer, or where girts join plates, and where one part of the sill joins another part of the sill.

*DOVETAIL* This is a special mortise and tenon. The tenon is tapered to fit tightly into a corresponding mortise. This is the strongest joint for joining two timbers at right angles. We use it to join the summer to the girts or plates.

*HALF-DOVETAIL* This joint looks, appropriately enough, like half a dovetail. It is used to join collar ties to the rafters. It is also used sometimes to join the members of the sill at the corners, or to join a corner brace to a post and girt or plate.

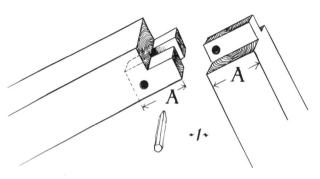

*MODIFIED MORTISE* This joint is used to join the rafter pairs at the roof peak.

*BIRDSMOUTH* The mortise in this joint is a V-shaped notch on the end of a rafter which either a) rests on the plate, or b) fits into a corresponding notch in the plate if an overhang is desired. Sometimes half of the portion resting on the plate is visible from the floor below.

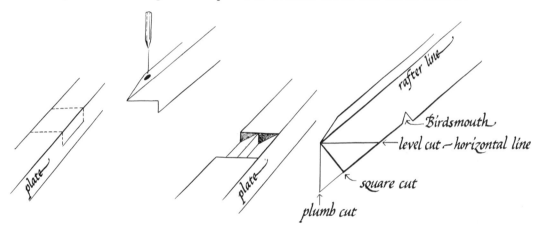

*OVERLAYING* Timbers are joined end to end and rest on timbers without the use of mortises and tenons. This system of joinery can save you time since the timbers are simply cut to proper length and the ends squared off. Overlaying is usually done when framing will not be exposed, or in an outbuilding.

*LETTING THROUGH* In this joint, the mortise literally goes all the way through the timber, and the other timber remains uncut. This system is sometimes used for joining joists and plates.

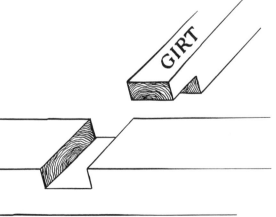

*SCARF JOINT* Scarf joints are used to join two timbers end to end so that they act as one uncut timber. The interlocking joint is self-supporting and therefore is used at points where there will be no supporting post beneath the joint.

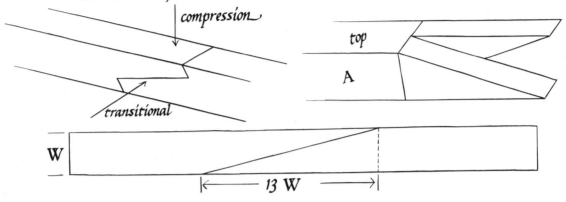

*VARIATIONS OF THE SCARF JOINT*

1) *true scarf*
2) *half-lap scarf* (This joint requires a supporting post.)
3) *halved scarf*

Like the definitions of the parts of the frame, these definitions are intentionally brief. They will become clearer to you as we describe how to cut the various joints. They will also help you to understand the terms we will be using as we go on to the considerations of the laying out and cutting of joints. Please remember that referring to the glossary as you are studying and building will help you to avoid mistakes.

## GENERAL CONSIDERATIONS FOR LAYING OUT AND CUTTING JOINTS

A properly executed joint will not weaken a timber. The old-timers who built by the seat of their pants always used to say that if you replace the wood you take out, the timber will not suffer for it. And, considering the physics of the situation, they were right. Look at a mortise which has been cut to make room for the tenon. Now, envision the forces which will be applied, that is, the weight of the materials themselves, and the load the timber must carry. Imagine how the top surface is trying to compress itself, thus reducing the dimensions of the notch. The bottom surface, under tension, is trying to pull itself apart. Now, if we replace this mortise, or fill it back up with a piece of wood, we can almost restore a timber to its natural state.

The forces can no longer try to reduce the dimensions of the mortise. They must, in fact, disperse themselves over a large area of the timber.

If, however, we put pieces of wood into mortises that were just slightly smaller than the pieces, the timber would begin to arch. Suppose, for example, we cut 16 notches and put back pieces that were 1/16 inch too big, the top dimension would then be 1 inch larger than the bottom. Of course, this does not actually happen because the wood becomes compressed. What does happen is that a stress force has been put on the top surface to offset the compressional force. This situation actually makes the timber stronger than it was in its uncut state, since an arch is created.

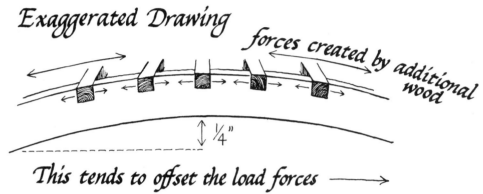

*Exaggerated Drawing*  *forces created by additional wood*

$\frac{1}{4}''$

*This tends to offset the load forces* ⟶

The unnatural forces applied to the frame while it is being raised are incredible. It is being pushed, pulled, dropped, hammered, mauled, temporarily braced, driven into place, straightened out, used as staging for the next bent, or as a crane for lifting timbers to the second and third stories and roof. When the frame is finally in place and properly braced, the processes of sheathing, decking, trimming out, plastering and the completion of other finishing stages add more and more material and mass. And yet, the frame is strong enough to bear all this. Consider the attack of the hammer alone. The swing of an ordinary hammer on a nail is 1000 pounds per square inch for the instant that it hits the nail! The combined forces exerted by the people living in the house and the climate outside it are not as great as the stresses it endures during construction. As the old-timers used to say, if the joints will hold together while the frame is being raised, they will be strong enough for anything that follows.

As we stated earlier, early builders made a continual effort to restore the original strength of the timber. Consequently, we have uncovered joints made one and even two hundred years ago that are still good and tight. The builders responsible for these joints had the kind of intuition that distinguishes the craftsman from the mechanic.

The house frame is like a piece of furniture. (In fact, as we explained in Chapter 1, the same joints used in good furniture making are simply greatly enlarged for the timber frame.) Both a fine deacon's bench and a timber frame reflect the skill of the craftsman, who has understanding of the complex forces which these structures must resist and who has a desire to create a finished, exposed product that is both functional and beautiful.

To achieve this kind of strength and quality, there are several important considerations in laying out and drawing the lines for all of these joints prior to cutting.

### Organization

*STACKING* Your timbers and other lumber should be stacked in piles by size and length. Use 1" x 2" boards to separate layers of timbers and leave spaces between all timbers so that air can circulate throughout the pile.

Stack all of your joists in one pile, all your posts in another, and so on. The timbers should be accessible, and be arranged so that you have room to maneuver around the piles, and so that they are as close as possible to the site. Tools should also be organized and kept close at hand. It is convenient to have a covered box in which you can store tools overnight.

*CHOOSING THE LOCATION FOR JOINTS ON A TIMBER* For each timber, a decision must be made as to which face or faces you will want exposed in the finished house. We think of the timbers as "living," having complexions and coloring and textures, or grains. Thus, part of your decision can be governed by aesthetic preference, and part by structural considerations. Most timbers have a crown, or convex curve. The crown can curve slightly or be quite bowed. A slight crown is desirable since arched timbers, as we mentioned before, are stronger than straight ones. On a timber which will lie horizontally, the joints should be laid out so that the crown will be on the top of the timber. A timber which will stand vertical is usually shorter than one used in a horizontal position, and thus the position of the crown is less critical. You can ignore it altogether on a post. Knots are weak points in a timber and they can cause the timber to twist in the completed frame. Knots also interfere with the proper cutting of joints. Interestingly enough, our forbears used to cut the knots out of their timbers, which really didn't help at all. Avoid cutting a joint, if possible, on a timber face which has large knots. However, if you are cutting a major, horizontal timber which has both a large knot and a pronounced crown, it is more important that the knot, rather than the crown, be on the top face of the timber.

We want to stress again that it is important to think of the frame in all stages of its development as part of the finish work. What you mark and cut on a timber eventually will relate to the markings and cuttings of some other timbers that will join it, and then to the finished interior. Think of the joint as "contained" in the rough, uncut dimensions of the timber. It is only for you to uncover it. It was Michelangelo who said that sculpture is simply a matter of taking away the excess.

### Measurement Definitions

To develop a consistent system of measuring and laying out a joint, there are some terms, numbers and relationships you will always need to know for each joint. It will help to refer to the labeled drawing.

*WIDTH OR SIDE* This refers to the larger dimension of a given timber, that is, the width or side of a 8" x 12" timber is 12 inches.

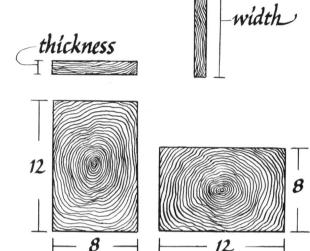

*THICKNESS* This refers to the smaller dimension of a given timber (8 inches in the example).

*LENGTH* This is the measurement from one end of a timber to the other.

*INSIDE DIMENSION* This is a measurement of the distance between two parallel timbers to be joined by a third.

*OUTSIDE DIMENSION* This is a measurement of the distance between two parallel timbers to be joined, and includes the thickness of the timbers themselves.

*CENTER LINE* This measurement is found by locating the line running down the middle of a face or end of a timber or joint.

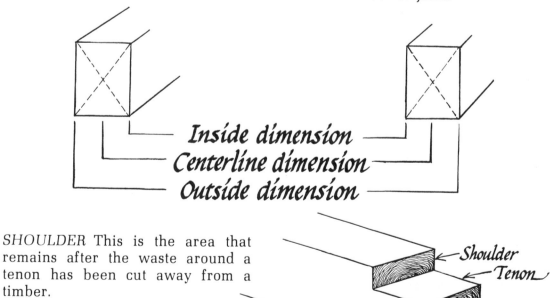

*SHOULDER* This is the area that remains after the waste around a tenon has been cut away from a timber.

*HAUNCH* This refers to the part of the whole timber beyond the shoulder which is to be let into another timber.

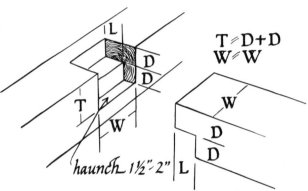

### Procedures and Relationships

1. All measurements for any given joint should be accurately figured and written down.

2. Develop a consistent pattern or sequence for measuring and cutting joints. This is important because timber sizes can be irregular and humans can be inaccurate. For example, either decide always to cut the tenons first and the mortises second, or the mortises first and the tenons second. We recommend cutting the tenons first and then the mortises to match. Otherwise, you are trying to measure a void. Also, by cutting the tenon first, you can, in many instances, lay out the mortise simply by tracing the tenon's dimensions on the timber. For example, when you set the braces, which are small enough to hold in place, you can trace around the tenon to lay out the mortise on the post.

3. It helps to have the ends of each timber "squared off" to final, overall length. When we explain cutting specific joints, we will describe a system for marking and squaring off the timber as part of the whole process of cutting the joint. In the meantime, squaring off the timber end should be considered part of the system of cutting joints.

4. The reason for developing a system is to establish a consistent point of reference for yourself. On the summer, for example, we choose to start laying out between the girts and then proceed outward. On girts and plates, we choose the distance between the posts as a reference point and lay out toward the ends of the girts and plates, or center lines over the posts.

### Measurements

As an illustration of the measurements and relationships necessary for a consistent system of joint layout and cutting, we will show the summer timber joined to two parallel girts. The summer's dimensions are 8" x 12", the girts are 7" x 9" and they are 14 feet apart in the frame.

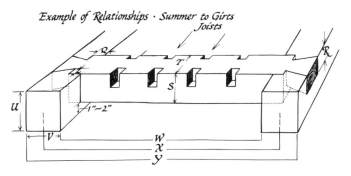

*Example of Relationships · Summer to Girts*

*Joists*

Overall length of summer = 14'7"

S = thickness of summer = 8"

T = width of summer = 12"

Z = 1/6 of T = 2"

V = thickness of girt = 7"

U = width of girt = 9"

W = inside dimension = 13'5"

X = center line dimension = 14'

Y = outside dimension = 14'7"

R = 1/2 thickness of summer = 4"

Q = 1½" haunch

(Shoulder to shoulder of dovetail = W + 2Q = 13'8")

The girts must be 1 to 2 inches thicker than the summer when all are in their final positions. One to 2 inches must remain below any joist housings on a summer, girt or plate. A post must provide a shoulder to all timbers that will rest upon it.

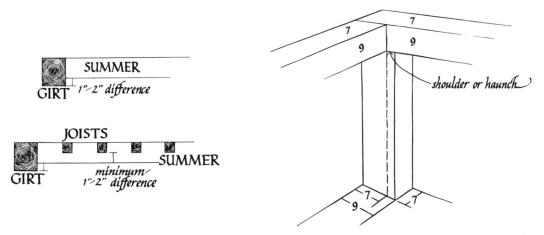

There are many exceptions to all of these rules, but here we have been dealing with the norm. In the next chapter, as we discuss laying out and cutting joints, all of these relationships will become even clearer. Remember that wood is the "prince" of building materials. It is strong, flexible, workable, and it takes a finish well. But most important of all, it is very forgiving.

# 7 LAYING OUT AND CUTTING JOINTS

The mortise and tenon form the basis for almost all joinery, and comprise the earliest joinery system known. The mortise and tenon joint was crudely cut in the Stone Age some six thousand years ago. Most other joints are variations on this theme. For example, the dovetail joint has a special tenon located on the top side of the timber rather than encased within it. It is important to learn, first of all, how to cut a basic mortise and tenon.

## TOOLS

You will need the following tools for laying out and cutting joints:

> framing square
> framing chisels (2 inches, 1½ inches and 1 inch)
> carpenter's mallet
> hand saw (6 or 8 point)
> broad hatchet
> combination square
> rule
> circular saw (if using power)
> chain saw
> rabbet plane
> carpenter's pencil
> corner chisel

# LAYING OUT AND CUTTING A CENTRAL AND FULL-WIDTH TENON

The degree of stress, strain, weight and pull a joint must withstand in a finished frame will determine whether your posts require a full-width tenon or a central tenon. A full-width tenon is the stronger of the two, and should be used in situations where the stress is exerted both by downward weight and from lateral pull. For example, the full-width tenon is used to join the major posts to the sills, girts and plates, and to join the rafters at the ridge. The distinctive difference between the full-width tenon and mortise, and the central tenon and mortise is that the full-width joint is usually pegged upon installation. The joint must be accessible in order to install the necessary trenail after it is assembled.

A central tenon is also used to join posts to sills, girts and plates, but for the most part, it is used in intermediate positions where the main forces are ones of compression. In the days before nails were widely used, a central tenon was also used for each stud to join it to the sills, girts and plates. This joint is mainly used to hold an upright in place.

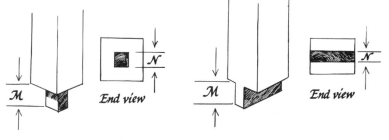

## Using Hand Tools

*SQUARING OFF*  It is important that the ends of each timber are squared off.

1. Mark a "squaring-off" line on each surface of the timber with a framing square, making sure that all four lines meet.

2. Make these marks as close to the rough end as possible so that you don't waste wood. Later on, when you make these cuts, be sure to cut straight through all four lines.

3. Using the framing square, mark and measure the length of the tenon on all four sides of the timber. The length of the tenon will be half the width of the timber receiving it. For example, using a 6" x 8" sill, the tenon on the post would be 4 inches long.

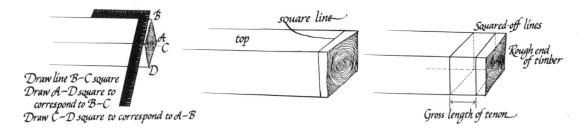

To mark the width of the tenon, set the combination square to dimension "N." The width of the tenon will be one-third the width of the timber having the tenon. If the timber is 6 inches wide, the tenon would be 2 inches. Connect the lines drawn in Step 2 with those drawn in Step 1 at point N.

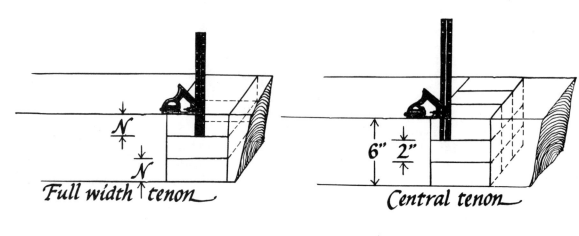

*Full width tenon*                     *Central tenon*

### CUTTING THE TENON

1. With a saw, cut out the excess. First, make the squaring-off cut. If you are cutting cross grain, use a cross cut saw, or if you can manage it, a bucksaw. If you are cutting with the grain, use a six point or rip saw. Of course, a chain saw cuts with the highest degree of efficiency.

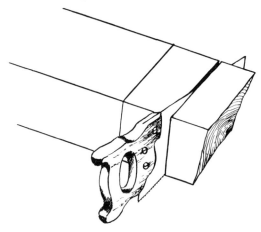

2. Continue the lines you marked in Step 3 (above) so that they connect on the end you just squared off. Then, saw the tenon.

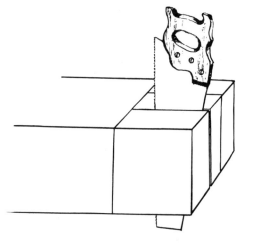

3.  To make a central tenon, rotate the timber and make two more cuts.

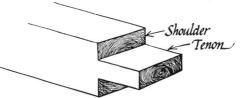

4.  Cut the shoulders.

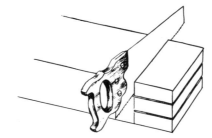

5.  If you are cutting a full-width tenon, clean out the corners with a chisel.

6.  If you are cutting a central tenon, rotate the timber and make the additional cuts on the other two sides for the shoulder.

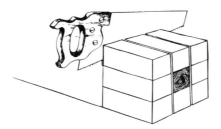

7.  Clean out the waste with a chisel.

**Using Electric Power**

1.  Proceed as in the squaring-off section with Steps 1 and 2.

2.  For Step 3, instead of setting distance "N" on the combination square, set a circular saw to cut to a depth of that distance. Make saw kerfs, or slices, 1 to 1½ inches apart. Using our example you would set the saw for a 2 inch deep cut. Then, rotate the timber and repeat the kerfs on the other side.

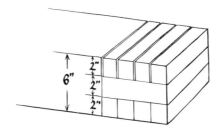

3. Clean out the waste with a broad hatchet or framing chisel for the full-width tenon.

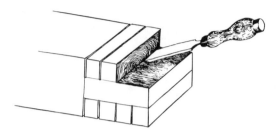

4. To make a central tenon, repeat Step 3 on the remaining two faces and clean out the excess wood as before.

### Special Uses of the Framing Square

Up to this point, we have presented the traditional techniques for laying out a tenon. However, there are shortcuts which will save you time and help you to standardize your system. Learning to use a framing square is one shortcut. The framing square blade is 2 inches wide. Lay the blade flush to the timber edge and make a mark. Do the same thing on each edge. Since you will always be making a mark 2 inches from any given edge, the sizes of the tenons will vary according to the timber size. Thus, the tenon will always be 4 inches (2" + 2") narrower than the overall width of the face. For example, a 7" x 7" post would have a 3 inch wide tenon. If you use a 6" x 8" post, the tenon will be 4 inches wide. If we had used the traditional method, the tenon would have been 2.3 inches wide on the 7" x 7" post. As you can see, this would be a more difficult measurement to lay out and cut.

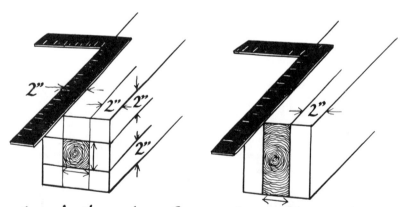

*Actual dimension of tenon is now the result of measuring out the waste— e.g. 7"x7" or 7" less 4"= 3" tenon*

### LAYING OUT AND CUTTING MORTISES

The first step in laying out and cutting a mortise is to choose the areas of the timber which are to house the tenons. Again, it is important to keep in mind which surfaces, if any, will be exposed, and the load the timbers will be carrying, and the location of crown and knots.

### Mortise for Central Tenon

1.  On the surface that will receive the tenon, mark out the dimension of the post.

2.  Locate the center point of these post dimensions by drawing the two diagonals.

3.  Measure the finished dimensions of the tenon and locate them on the layout for the post, using the center point as your point of reference. These lines, drawn on both sides of the center point, should be equidistant and parallel from the point to the lines representing the dimensions of the post.

4.  Using a drill bit equal to the thickness of the tenon, bore to a point deep enough to receive the tenon.

5.  With a framing or mortising chisel, clean out the waste, so that the hole to receive the square tenon is square.

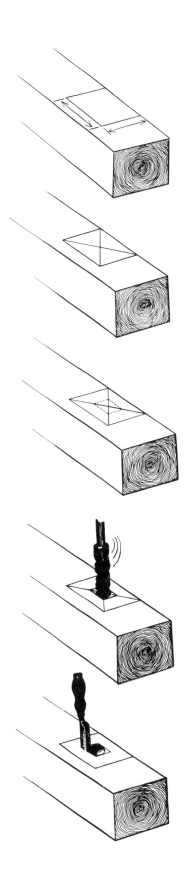

### Mortise for a Full-Width Tenon

1.  Proceed as you would for a central tenon by marking out the dimensions of the post. Here are two examples of several possible mortise locations.

    (a)  on a horizontal timber
    (b)  on a vertical timber

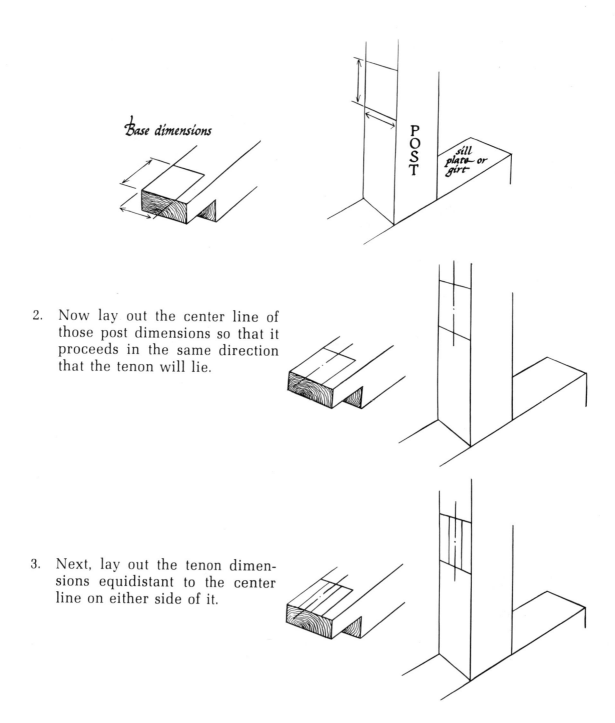

2.  Now lay out the center line of those post dimensions so that it proceeds in the same direction that the tenon will lie.

3.  Next, lay out the tenon dimensions equidistant to the center line on either side of it.

4. With a drill bit equal to the thickness of the tenon, bore a pocket deep enough to receive the tenon. With practice, you will find that the tenon will fit the mortise more easily if the mortise is cut just a shade larger than the measured dimensions. This small measurement is really indefinable, and is known in the trade as a "hair." Clean out the waste as you did before.

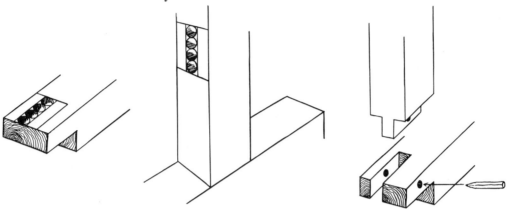

## Special Uses of the Framing Square

When laying out the mortise with a framing square, it is not necessary to find center lines. Simply use the blade of the square to measure 2 inches from each edge of the base dimensions of the post.

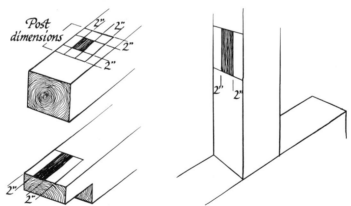

## SPECIAL SITUATIONS

When a mortise and tenon joint is used to secure a girt to a post, there are often other girts entering at the same place. You must consider the order in which you will assemble the joints since this may affect the length of a tenon and the corresponding depth of a mortise. The drawing to the right illustrates the order of assembly.

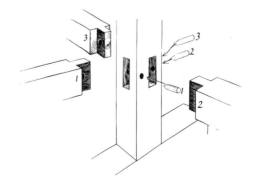

In any multiple joint situation, the length of the tenon is still determined by the basic rule, but with some changes. When three girts enter a post in the same area, you can either shorten the tenons a hair, or set the mortises slightly off center.

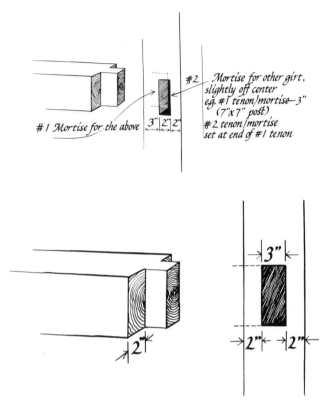

Again, we emphasize that every step in the process of cutting and joining is important in relation to the total frame.

The framing square can be used to make the adjustments in this multiple joint situation. The tenon can be made shorter and the mortises shallower. For example, if you are joining a 7" x 7" post to 7" x 9" girts, make the tenon 2 inches long and the mortise a corresponding depth.

This shortcut is both accurate and time-saving. No matter what the dimensions of the timber are, the tenon will always fit the mortise, given a reasonable amount of skill in cutting the tenon. The constancy of the framing square helps to reduce human error. You always must keep in mind how much wood you can take away and still have a timber that can do the work of joining and supporting, so make sure that you don't cut away too much. For example, if a post is 5" x 5" and you use the 2 inch blade of the framing square to determine the width of the tenon, the tenon would only be 1 inch wide. This size tenon is not large enough to do the job. However, if you use the 1½ inch tongue of the square instead, this would leave a 2 inch tenon, which is adequate. The 1 inch blade of a combination square would be a good constant measure for the tenon of a 4" x 4" post.

## FINAL STEP FOR ALL METHODS

The final step for preparing any tenon to be inserted in a mortise is to chamfer, or shave off, the edges of the tenon. You should do this as a precautionary measure, since it is difficult to pull a joint apart once it is assembled. The tenon might not fit because of some small piece of wood left in the bottom of the mortise. It can be disheartening to see how much trouble one small piece of shaving, or a ragged edge can cause.

*Corners have been "knocked off"*
## CHAMPHERED

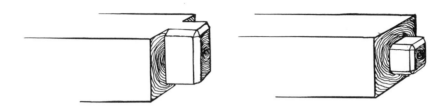

## LAYING OUT AND CUTTING A HALF-LAP JOINT

The half-lap joint consists of an L-shaped tenon notched out of the end of a timber and a corresponding L-shaped mortise in the receiving timber. Following are some formulas for determining the length of the tenon.

1. When joining a joist to a girt or plate, the length of the tenon is one-half the thickness of the receiving timber.

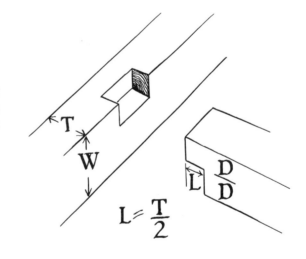

2. When joining one sill timber to another, or one plate to a girt at a corner, the length of the tenon is equal to the thickness of the receiving timber.

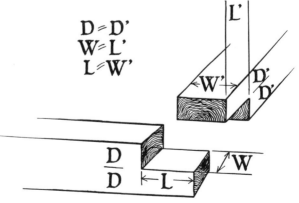

3. When two sections of the sill are joined end to end, the length of the tenon is equal to the length of the mortise.

This situation does not necessarily occur in every frame.

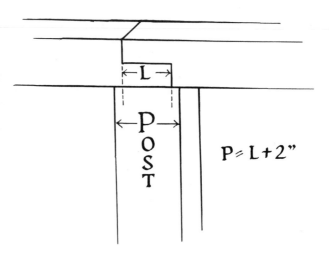

4. When two sections of a plate are joined end to end, the post beneath must be 2 inches wider than the length of the lap. If it is not possible to have a post 2 inches wider, then it is necessary to shorten the lap so that the joint is adequately supported by the post.

$$P = L + 2''$$

5. Here are some examples of joining joists on both sides of a timber.

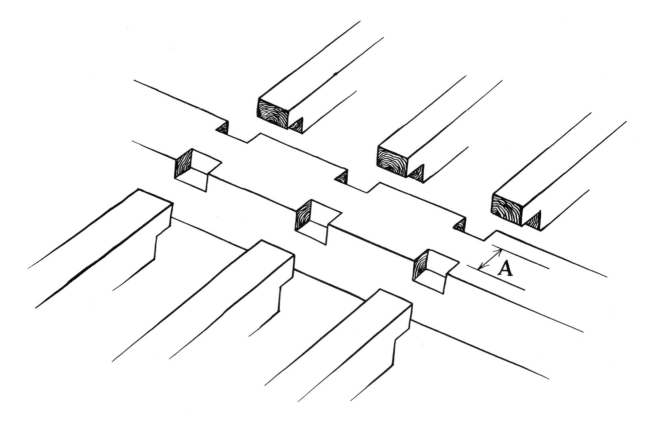

The lap must be at least 3 inches long. However, you must make some judgments before deciding to use any of the preceding rules. The situation of joists coming into both sides of a timber usually occurs on a summer or chimney girt. Both of these timbers must span a long, unsupported distance. There must be enough wood left between the mortises (distance "A" above) so that these large timbers are not weakened. For instance, if we were to apply the rule that the lap, or tenon, be one-half the thickness of the receiving timber to the case of an 8" x 12" summer, we would find that the summer would not have enough wood left, after a 6 inch mortise was cut away, to enable it to bear its load. So we would make the tenon 3 inches long. If joists are being joined on both sides of this summer, it is obvious that 6 inch mortises on both sides would definitely not leave an adequate amount of wood. Therefore, the rule in this situation is that the distance between the mortises (distance "A") must be at least 6 inches.

6. When one large major timber joins another, for example, if you are joining a girt to a plate, or a summer to a girt, you may need a mortise that spans the entire thickness of the timber. This joinery is called "letting through."

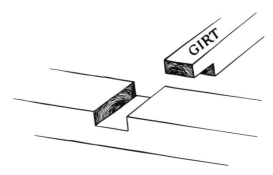

### Laying Out and Cutting the Lap

The half-lap tenon is one of the easiest joints to cut. First, decide what length the tenon will be.

1. Mark the squaring-off line.

2. Determine which surface of the timber will be the top, and decide whether the lap is to be on the top or the bottom of the timber. Next, find the center of the timber's side (D).

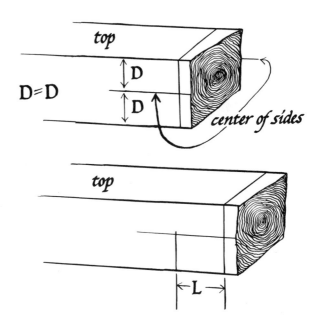

3. Measure the length of the lap (L) from the squaring-off line.

4.  If the lap is located on the top of the timber, turn the timber over so that the portion to be cut away is more accessible. We always mark the portion to be removed with an "X." It helps us to distinguish clearly between what is to be removed and other layout markings.

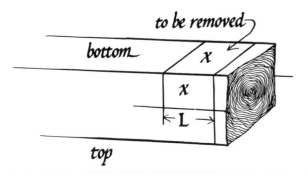

5.  If you are using hand tools, saw the squaring-off line.

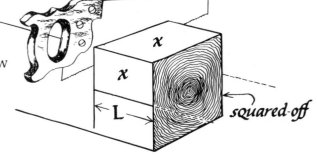

6.  You may make several saw kerfs to depth and then chisel or axe out the necessary portion. Or, use a rip saw to saw from the squared-off end to the initial depth cut. Then use a broad hatchet.

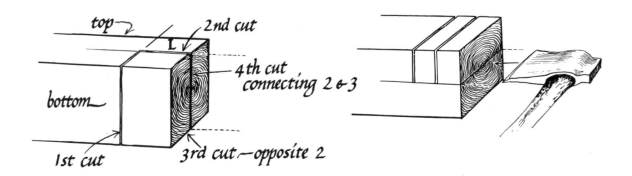

If a power circular saw is available, make the square cut as usual, and then make the length and depth cuts. Turn the timber on its side and saw down the center line to the tenon length on both sides. Finally, saw down the square end, if necessary, to connect the two side cuts.

7.  The remaining portion can be knocked out easily and cleaned up with a hatchet or chisel.

### Laying Out and Cutting the Mortise

These mortises are basically prepared in the same way as the other mortises we have discussed. When joists are joined to girts, plates or summers, they are usually spaced 12 to 30 inches apart, on center. It is important, therefore, to lay out all the centers for all the mortises before laying out in detail any individual one. The half-lap mortise is cut out on the edge of a timber. This location makes the mortise more accessible both for boring out with a bit, and for cutting with a hand or circular saw.

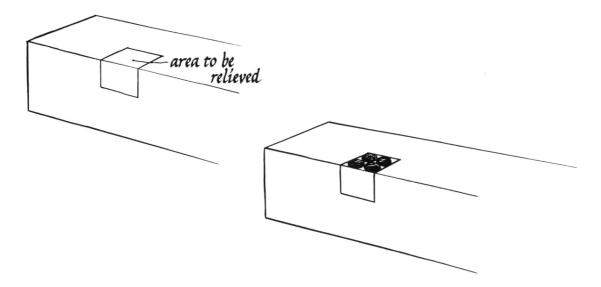

Clean out the pocket with a framing chisel. Again, this process is made much easier by the fact that you can approach the joint from both sides.

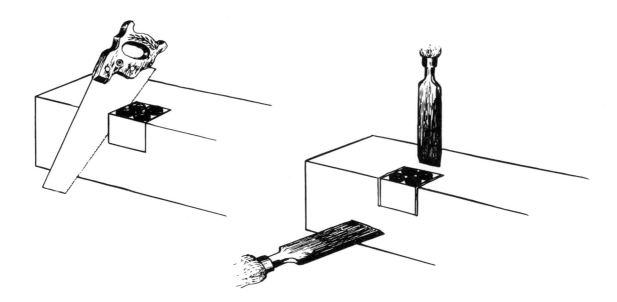

### Special Situations

There are some modifications to the simple half-lap just as there are for any joint. First, when a half-lap is being used over a corner post, the traditional method is to cut two small tenons on the top of the post to tie the three timbers together. A corresponding mortise would then be cut in each of the two lapped timbers.

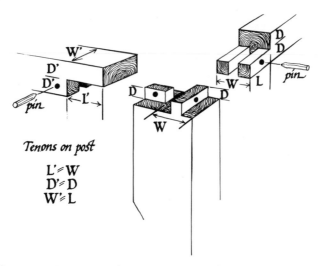

*Tenons on post*

$$L' \not= W$$
$$D' \not= D$$
$$W' \not= L$$

For the sake of convenience and consistency, the tenons in this situation would be equal to the depth of the lap.

A second modification of the half-lap joint occurs when three major pieces, for example, two plates and a girt, are to be joined over a post. Proceed as you would for the half-lap over the corner post, being aware, however, that the plates must share a tenon on the post. The laps, therefore, must be one-half the normal length. The girt would have a mortise to house the smaller tenon on the post.

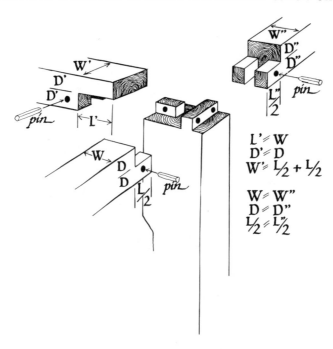

$$L' \not= W$$
$$D' \not= D$$
$$W' \not= L/2 + L/2$$

$$W \not= W''$$
$$D \not= D''$$
$$L/2 \not= L''/2$$

## THE HAUNCHED HALF-LAP JOINT

The haunched half-lap joint is simply a regular half-lap with a modified mortise. With the haunched half-lap, it is very important to plan ahead. You will be increasing the inside dimension of this timber when you cut the haunch. Therefore, when you select a timber to use, it must be long enough to accommodate the haunches and still span the necessary distance between the timbers. As an example, let's say the haunches are to be 1½ inches on either end of the timber. The uncut timber, then, must be 3 inches longer than the final inside dimensions will be.

Recall the example of the relationship of the summer to girt: the inside dimension of the stick would be the length shoulder to shoulder.

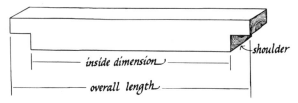

1. Special attention must be paid to the layout of a haunch tenon. The mortise is simply a half-lap equal to the length of the haunch, cut into the receiving timber.

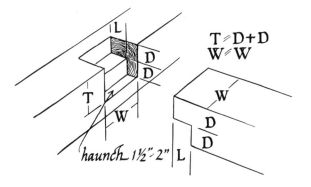

2. The tenon's overall width and thickness are also laid out. It is helpful to lay out the line that represents the bottom of the lap as a guide for both boring and chiseling. To relieve the mortise, proceed as you would for a simple mortise. First, saw out the lines. Then bore out the waste. Be careful with this step, since the depths differ. Also, it is advisable to bore in from the side rather than from the top.

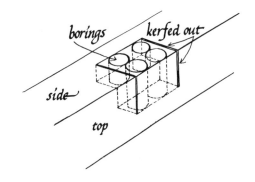

3. Clean out the mortise with the framing or mortising chisel.

## LAYING OUT AND CUTTING A DOVETAIL JOINT

A dovetail joint is used primarily to join the summer timber to other major timbers, such as a plate and girt. The dovetail shape insures that the joint is so secure that a trenail is not needed. The complete haunch of the dovetail rests inside the mortise. Thus, the tenon is as long as the receiving timber is wide.

### Laying Out and Cutting the Tenon

The dovetail is an example of a haunched half-lap. Its layout is basically the same. It is used, however, quite differently. It is generally used to join much larger and heavier timbers. Therefore, it is important that dovetails fit the first time around, because once you start to raise a summer, it is difficult to move, much less remove, the joint. We choose again to cut the tenon first and to use its measurements for the layout of the mortise. Using the measurements of one part of a joint to determine the size of the other part is a good way to check your overall layout. Many small inaccuracies can develop from tools that are slightly out of square, pencil lines of different thicknesses, and timber dimensions that vary.

1.  Choose your stock, locate possible crowns, determine which surfaces to expose, and check the overall length of the timber. Then, lay out the haunched half-lap. The tenon length is the full width of the timber into which it will be mortised *less* the dimension of the haunch. For example, if a girt were 7" x 9", the tenon would be 5½ inches with a 1½ inch haunch.

2.  Lay out the dovetail on the top surface. We choose to use the 2 inch blade of the framing square to determine the taper if the summer is thicker than 8 inches. If the thickness is just around 8 inches, we use the 1½ inch tongue. Make a mark at the point where the 1½ inch tongue or 2 inch blade meets the mark that corresponds to the length of the lap (A). Connect this point to the end of the lap at the squaring-off line (B).

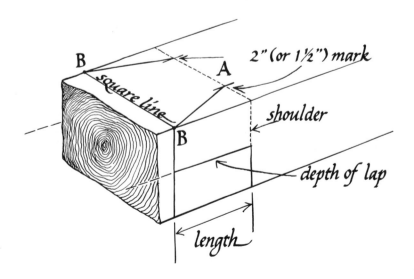

3. Proceed first by cutting the depth, the length, and the squaring-off lines. Make the two dovetail cuts, stopping at the shoulder.

4. Set your saw to a depth of 1½ or 2 inches and cut the shoulder, stopping at the dovetail line. You can use a hand saw.

5. Take out the waste left from squaring off. Clean out both the lap and the wedge up to the shoulder.

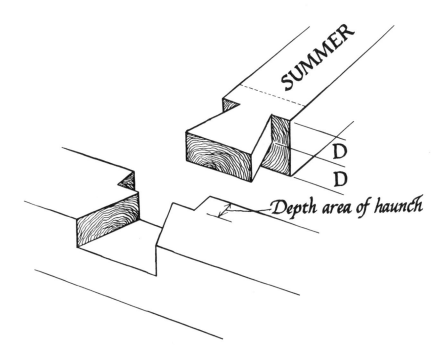

### Laying Out and Cutting the Mortise

The mortise of the dovetail joint is much like the mortise of any haunched half-lap.

1. Determine the location of the mortise on the timber and use the dimensions of the tenon to mark out the entire half-lap and haunch. Then lay out the depth of the haunch, the 1½ or 2 inch dovetail, and the depth of the lap.

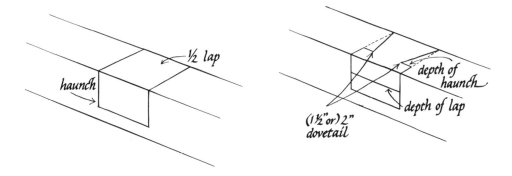

In all joinery, it is important to imagine the joint inside the mortise
before you begin to remove any of
the waste. If you can envision this, it
becomes easier to see what and how
much must be removed.

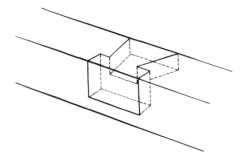

2.  If you will be using a circular
    saw, first set it to the proper
    depth and saw the dovetails. In
    this case, you can saw right
    through and not worry about the
    shoulder, since it is going to be
    removed anyway.

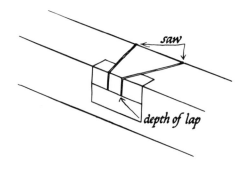

3.  Then set the saw for the depth of
    the haunch and *very* carefully
    cut the haunch lines out.
    (Disregard this step if you do not
    use a circular saw. This par-
    ticular cut requires "burying"
    the saw by lifting the guard, and
    is only recommended for ex-
    perienced carpenters.)

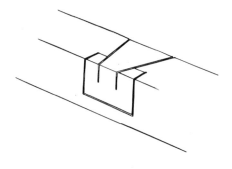

4.  Next, bore out the remaining por-
    tions of the joint to proper depth.

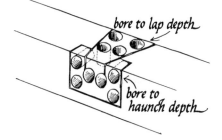

5.  Finally, use a framing chisel to cut out the remaining portion of wood and to clean the pocket out. Start with the haunch area and move to the lap area.

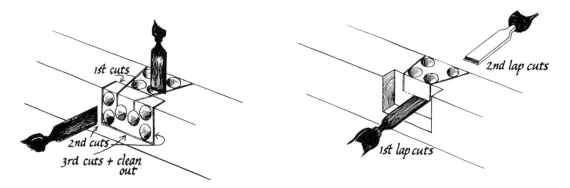

6.  Before bringing the joint home, make sure that the mortise is clean and that the inside corners of the dovetail are champhered so the tenon does not become obstructed.

## THE SCARF JOINT

The strength of the scarf joint approximates as nearly as possible the strength of a whole, uncut timber. The degree of strength will depend on which scarf joint is used. The simple scarf joint, which is not used in timber work, must be glued and screwed. It is generally used for boat masts and furniture. For this kind of work, the length of the scarf is 13 times the width of the lumber, making it impractical for framing.

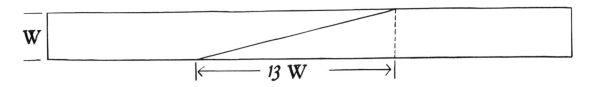

For timber framing, the traditional true scarf joint, the halfed scarf, and the double splayed scarf (which is a modification of the halved scarf) are the most frequently used scarf joints. These three vary in their applications and complexity. All are unable to resolve the tensile forces naturally and therefore rely on bolts or pegs to keep them from being pulled apart.

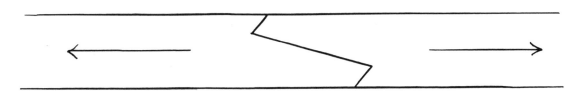

They all resist compressive forces, and the latter two resist transitional forces to a greater degree than the first.

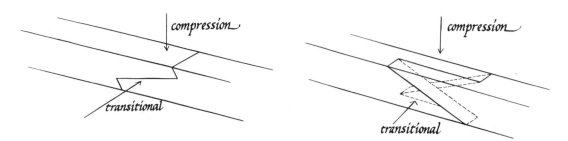

The only two scarf joints that resist compression, transition and tensile forces are the tabled scarf joint and the double tenoned scarf. Both require wedges, which, in effect, "pre-stress" the joint.

The layout for all these joints is basically the same. First, make a decision about which joint to use, considering the forces it is to resist, the size of the timbers being used, and the location of the joint in the house. Second, locate the center line of the joint with respect to the overall length of the timbers being joined. We will use the halved scarf as an example since it incorporates portions of both the true and double splayed scarf joints.

1.  The overall length of the scarf, 2x, depends on the size of the timber. A ratio of three to four times the width will serve as a good formula for determining this length. Therefore, with an 8" width and ratio of three, the overall length is 24 inches for the scarf (x would equal 12 inches). Each timber, then, must be 1 foot longer than the distance it is to span. In our example, Timber A plus Timber B is a span of 20 feet and the center line of the joint occurs at a point 9 feet from the end. Therefore, we need one timber to be 10 feet long and the other to be 12 feet long.

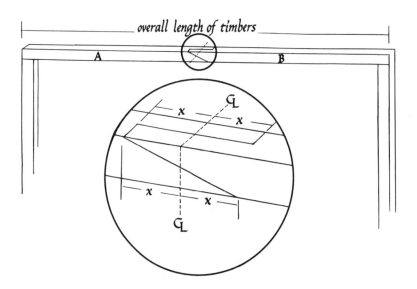

2.  One-half the length of the scarf is measured on either side of the center line. Lay out the depth of the scarf, which is one-half the thickness of the timber.

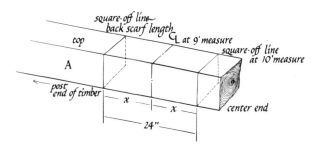

3.  Lay this center line out on both top and bottom, using a combination square. Finally, lay out the diagonal line on the sides of the timber. Mark inside from top post end to bottom center end of timber first, and then mark on the outside. Just reverse from the bottom end to top center end.

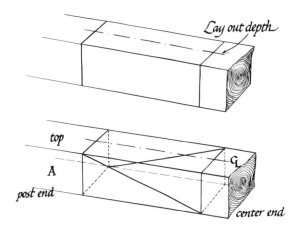

4.  To relieve the waste, simply saw the diagonals to the center of the thickness, rip (saw) down the thickness line to the diagonal line and remove.

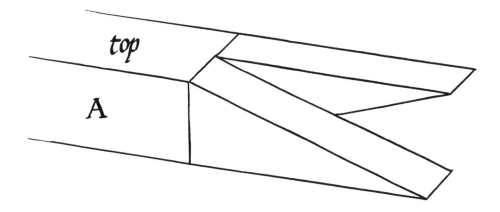

The matching timber, B, is approached in much the same way. The difference is in the length of the timber, and the joint is just the opposite.

## A FINAL STEP FOR ALL JOINTS

Because rough timbers are generally oversized, it is very important to box the joints where needed. Often some portion of the joint will need to be shaved or planed down before final assembly. Otherwise, if the joint is too large in any of its parts, other portions of the joint will be spread apart and enlarged. For example, a 7" x 9" girt may in fact measure 7½" x 9". If the measurements for a tenon are based on a 7 inch thickness, some portions of the joint will be too large. Therefore, always check these critical dimensions and make alterations if you find they are incorrect.

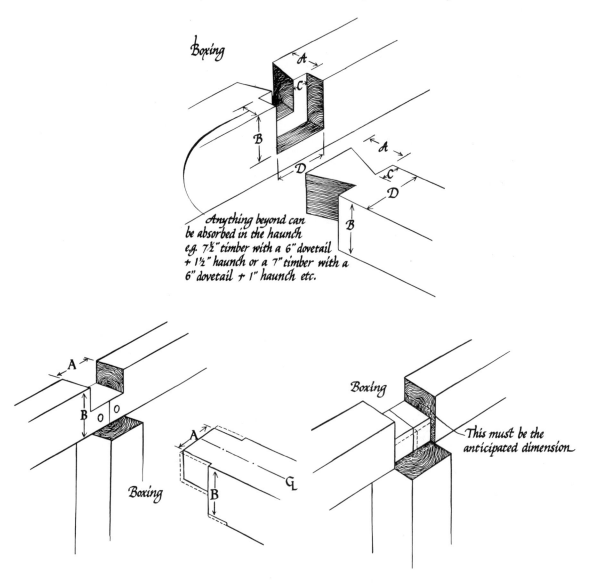

There are, of course, many other joints used in timber framing. With the joints we have discussed, however, you should be able to frame a house. Any other joinery you might use will be modifications of the joints we have discussed. You will be able to make these joints fit your specific needs at your building site.

# 8 LAYING OUT AND CUTTING BRACES

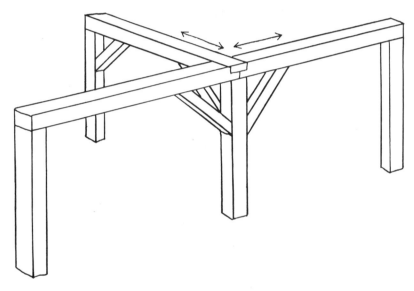

Braces are the smallest members of the timber frame, yet, because they help to make a structure able to withstand the forces of the wind, they are among the frame's most important members. When entire walls were composed of stone or masonry, braces were unnecessary because the mass of these structures made them resilient. Stone or masonry frames were braced by buttresses. When lighter wood frames were developed, some method for resisting wind pressure had to be developed. The carpenters borrowed a concept from shipwrights who used the "knee brace" to make their boats rigid. Knee braces were designed to conserve internal space, thus their use in buildings allowed for more floor and wall space, which in turn allowed for windows and doors.

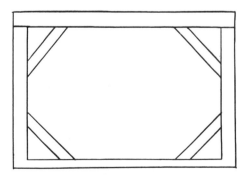

A structure must be both stable and rigid. To be considered stable, a structure must be immobile in respect to the earth. The live load of people and their possessions, and the dead load of the building itself, including a large chimney and fireplaces, are all downward forces which help to make a structure stable. The pull of gravity directs these forces downward along the posts to the foundation and the earth. To be considered rigid, a structure must be immobile in respect to itself. An unbraced rectangle, however heavy it might be, lacks rigidity. Its shape can easily change to a parallelogram without its dimensions changing.

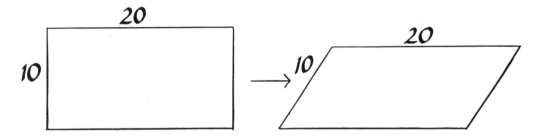

Compare an unbraced rectangle to a triangle. A triangle cannot change shape without at least one of its dimensions also changing. Braces create triangles which in turn create a rigid structure.

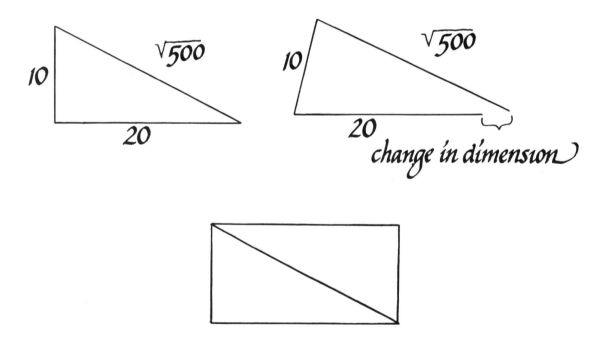

What we are bracing the frame against is the force of the wind, which can be extraordinary. The formula for determining this force is $P = .00256 \, v^2$, where P is the pressure against a surface in pounds per square foot, and v is the velocity of the wind in miles per hour. Thus a 50 mile per hour gust could apply 6.4 pounds per square foot. If you had a 17 foot wall that was 40 feet long, there would be 4,352 pounds of pressure against it, not including the pressure on the roof. Although this is a simplification of the total situation, it is clear that the frame somehow must withstand this degree of force. A 50 mile per hour gust tends to lift, twist, overturn, and/or bend the building, as well as press against it. A large structure such as a 30 or 40 foot timber frame weighs some 50,000 pounds and could withstand the 40,000 pounds of pressure and the 10,000 pounds of lift forces that are created by a hurricane. It is remarkable and somewhat ironic that with technological advances, builders can construct a prefab house in a factory, ship it down our roads and place it on a foundation without its developing a single crack in a window or the sheetrock, and then have the whole thing blow away in a bad storm because of its fundamental instability.

There are some general rules to observe regarding effective bracing. The brace should be about half as long as the posts, and placed at a 45 degree angle to the post. All the corner posts should be braced from the post to the plate or girt, and to the sill or plate or girt. It is important that braces are placed so that they oppose each other.

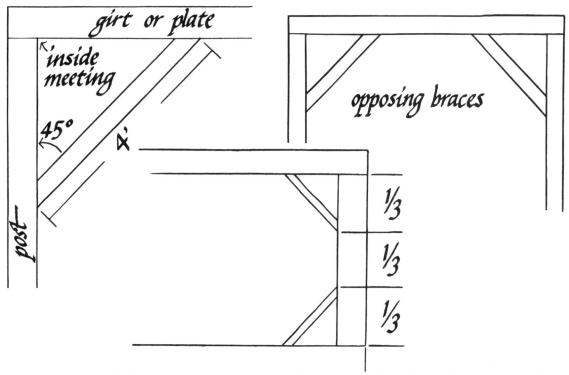

In a properly built roof system, one rafter braces the other. Though the rafter pairs push against each other, the pairs could still topple over. When king posts are used, braces can be placed from the post to the ridge. In a gambrel roof, braces can be placed from the posts to the girts. In a straight run gable roof, braces must be put between the rafters and purlins.

How you choose to cut your braces will be a decision which depends on the system you intend to use for raising. You can either let in the braces once the rest of the frame is raised, or you can join the braces to the posts and other timbers prior to raising each complete bent. If you let in the braces after the frame is raised, you can use a half-lap joint or nail or peg in a brace that has a flush cut at a 45 degree angle.

### Flush-Cut Braces

The simplest and most basic brace-cutting method is to cut 4" x 4" timbers to 4 foot overall lengths with opposing 45 degree cuts on each end. Use a combination square to lay out the 45 degree angle on one end. Draw square lines down the other two faces and connect all the lines on the back side. Then, measure down 4 feet from the longest point and lay out the 45 degree cuts in the opposite direction. Repeat the entire line-drawing process on the other side of the timber.

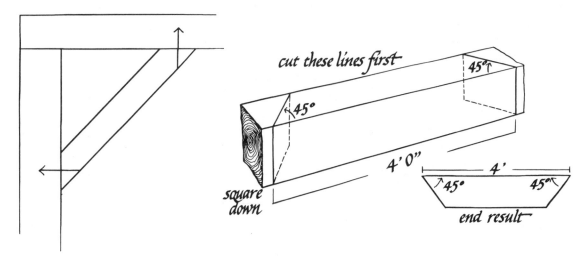

If you use a power circular saw to make the cuts, set the saw to its maximum depth and square cut the angle lines on one side. Then turn the piece over and match the cuts.

### Half-Lap Braces

Begin this brace as you would a flush-cut brace, by laying out the opposing 45 degree lines. Then, lay out the squaring-off lines on all four faces at both ends of the brace.

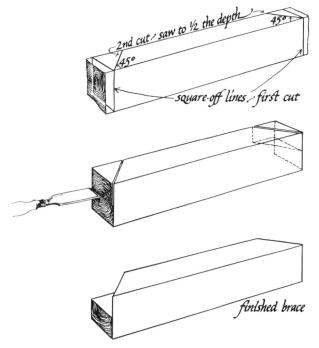

Next, make the square cuts off both ends. Then set the circular saw to a depth that measures one-half the thickness of the brace. Cut the angle lines. Finally, use a framing chisel to remove the small triangular pieces of wood.

### Half-Lap Variations

You can choose to use a longer tenon for the half-lap brace. This requires careful consideration of the angles so that you do not remove too much wood from either the post or girt. You can use the same cutting method. First, make the squaring-off cuts and all the full depth cuts. Then, make the one-half depth cuts and chisel out the waste.

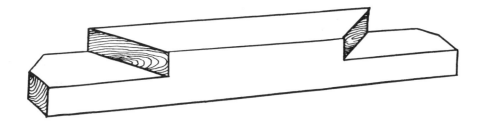

### Central Tenon Brace

If you choose to let in your braces before you raise the frame, and to include them in a bent, you will need a central tenon on your braces. To lay out the central tenon on the brace, follow the rules for determining thickness of tenons in Chapter 7 on page 32. The length of the tenon depends on the prescribed angles and dimensions of the braces.

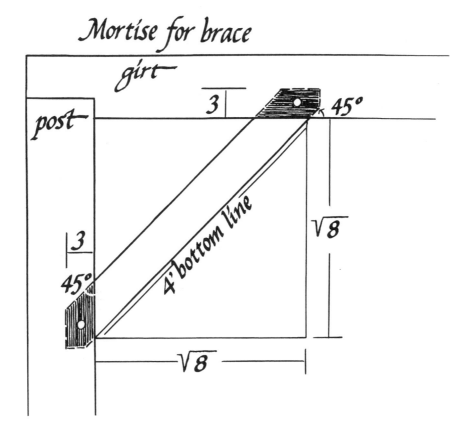

You will need corresponding mortises on the posts, girts, and plates. The dimensions of these mortises should be measured very accurately. Great care should also be taken in determining which posts will be braced, where those posts will be located, which will be in the corners, and which direction each post will be facing. Also, you must remember that boxing the timbers will vary the fittings by 1/4 to 1/2 inch and this can throw the whole frame out of square and plumb. Lastly, you must consider whether the braces will be flush with the inside of the post, the outside of the post, or be placed in the middle. Because of all these variables, we suggest that you cut the mortises on raising day when you can lay out the entire bent, and make all adjustments before you begin cutting.

If you do cut your mortises before raising day, some roof mathematics will help you to place the mortises on the posts, girts and plates. Since the brace creates a triangle, you can use the formula $a^2 + b^2 = c^2$ to determine the placement of the mortise. If "c" is the brace, we know that it measures 4 feet. We also know that a=b, since the post and girt join at right angles, and the brace is at a 45 degree angle to the post and girt. Therefore, $2a^2 = 16'$, and both a and b equal the square root of 8 feet. This will be the measurement from the intersection of the inside corner of the post and girt to the bottom of the mortise.

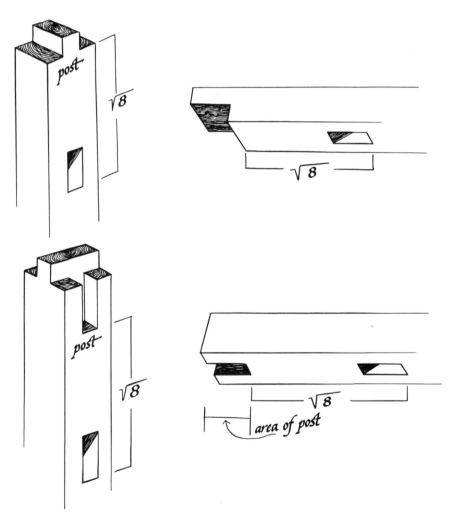

Next, locate the mortise and the correct angles within the thickness of the post and girt, either flush to the outside or inside, or placed somewhere in between. This is an aesthetic choice; you are determining how much of the brace you want exposed in your finished interior wall.

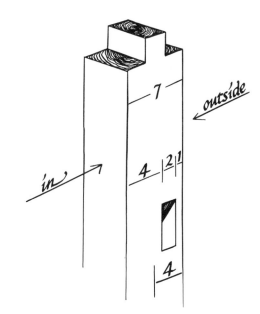

Lay out and cut the mortise so that it corresponds to the tenon.

Now that you have chosen a method for bracing your frame, we will describe how to raise and secure the braces, according to whichever method you used. In the case of the flush-cut brace, nail or peg the brace in place in the raised frame using 6 or 8 inch spikes, or oak pegs.

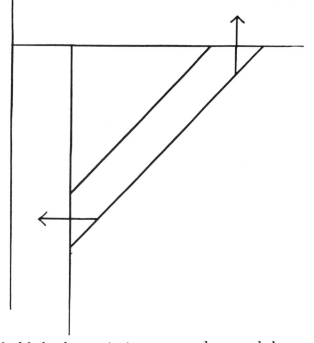

Always make sure that the lines for the pegs or spikes are at right angles to the post and girt.

If you are using a half-lap joint, hold the brace in its proper place and draw around, or scribe, the joint. Then notch out the mortise with a chisel. Use pegs or nails to secure the brace, being careful not to split the lap or drive all the way through the post.

To raise the bent including the braces, begin by laying out the bent, making all necessary adjustments for dimensions, boxing, and squareness. Do not peg the bent together. Lay the braces on the top surface of the bent and make marks at the intersection of the brace and the post and girt. Trace the dimensions of the tenon onto the post and girt surfaces.

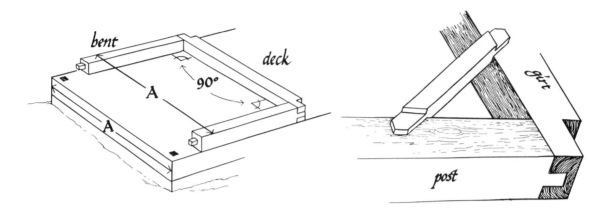

Make sure the shoulder cuts of the brace are in line with the face of the post and girt. Then set a combination square to the depth of the shoulder if the brace is to be flush to the outside of the building. Lay this line out on the appropriate faces of the post and girt. Next, lay out a second line so that it is parallel to the first, and equal to the thickness of the tenon. Finally, draw square lines down from the marks on the post and girt, and then relieve the waste.

To set these braces, angle the posts away from the girt at the bottom, and insert the brace. Pull the whole bent back to its final position, and peg the unit together, post to girt, and brace to post and girt. Carefully raise the bent.

### Cutting Pegs

The pegs, or trenails, are even smaller than the braces, but they, too, play a vital role in the structure of the timber frame.

Pegs are the fastening devices for securing the joinery of a timber frame. We prefer to make ours from oak. They vary in size according to the size of the members they are holding together. The diameter of the peg is related to the length of the tenon. Generally, the diameter of a peg is one-third the length of the tenon. For example, if the tenon is 3 inches long, the peg should be 1 inch in diameter. If it is a tusk tenon and the mortise is in a 7 inch timber, then the diameter of the peg should be 2¼ inches. A peg this large is called a trenail (pronounced tru-nl). If the tenon is 2 inches long, then the diameter of the peg should be 5/8 inches. A peg this small is usually called a pin.

The lengths of all these pegs depend on whether or not they will protrude from the timber once they are driven in place. If it is permissible for them to protrude because no other timber will be in the way, then they should be 2 inches longer than the thickness of the timber. Pegs for rafters, collar ties, most braces, corner joinery, scarf joints, and posts at sills should be longer than the thickness of the timber being pegged. Otherwise, they should only be as long as the timber is thick.

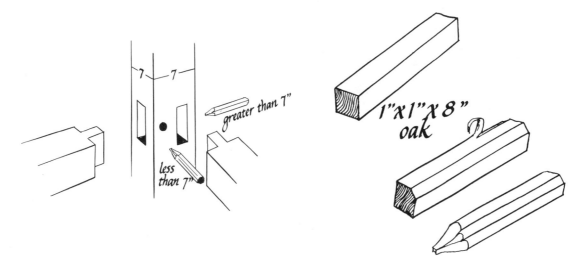

Now, let's talk about the hole for the peg. The corners of the square peg bind the peg permanently to the hole; thus it becomes, as in the old adage, "a square peg in a round hole." The holes for the pegs are bored on raising day, and should be just a hair smaller than the peg. Obviously, the peg cannot be completely square, (that is, equal to the diameter of the hole), or it wouldn't fit in the hole at all. So, to cut the 1 inch pegs, rip some 1 inch oak boards into 1" x 1" strips. Then cut these strips to proper length. With a hatchet or a plane, knock off the sharp corners, creating roughly the shape of an octagon. Finally, point the end of the peg slightly.

The alternative to this method is to borrow an old peg sizing machine. This is a piece of hard steel that has holes ranging from 1/2 inch to 2 inches drilled in it. After ripping down the oak boards, rough off the square corners and point the stock. Then as a final step, take a maul and drive the pegs through the appropriate size hole in the steel. This method will give you a very rough round peg.

The final step for cutting pegs, whether you use a peg sizing machine or not, is to make small cuts in the side of the peg with a hatchet or knife. These notches will prevent the peg from backing out.

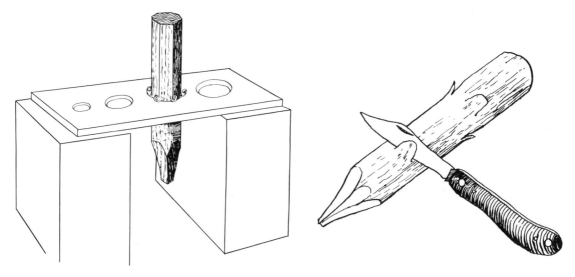

66

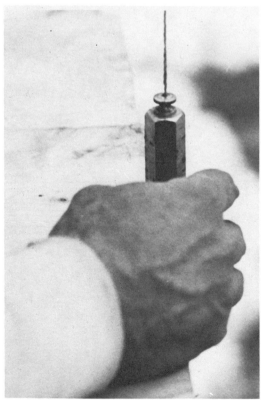

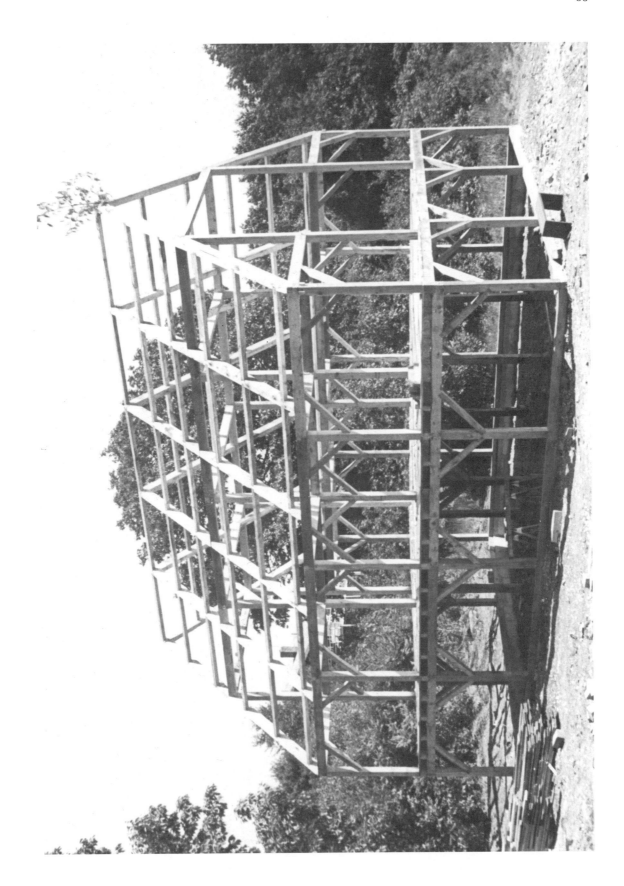

# 9 RAFTERS

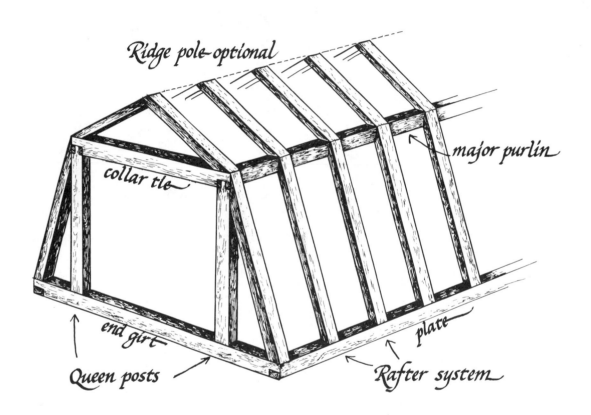

## FORCES

Rafters are unique members of the timber frame. They are the last timbers to be raised, and are as exposed as the other timbers in the finished house. In many respects, they are the timbers that work hardest in the frame. Because rafters slope, and because they must support a surface at the highest and least protected point of the house, they are subject to the most complex set of forces. By comparison, the other timbers in the frame support only vertical loads, loads which proceed straight down to the earth. Even additional posts, girts, plates and joists are merely stacked upon the ones beneath them and only add to the vertical force. The rafters, on the other hand, try to force the building apart at the plate. In a frame, then, there are two forces, operating perpendicular to one another, which at once try to spread the frame apart and press it down.

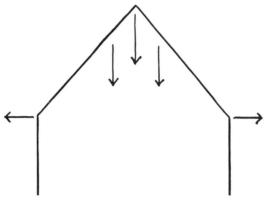

How, then, are these forces resolved? In a gable roof, each pair of rafters must form a triangle with the framing on which it rests. The attic floor framing may act as a tie between the feet. Or, a collar tie may be used to make the roof rigid.

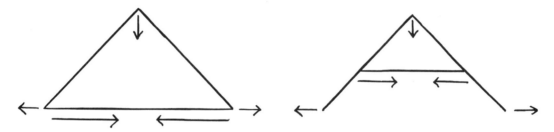

If the rafters in a house are short (for instance, if they are 12 feet) the builder probably would decide not to have an attic floor. In this situation, joists or girts would act as ties and resolve the spreading forces of the rafters. If the rafters in a house are longer, if they are between 16 feet and 20 feet and if they are small timbers, 5" x 7"s, then the collar ties would not only resolve the spreading forces, but also would provide support to prevent sagging from weight loads. In this case, there would also be floor framing for the attic. In a roof system using both long and large principal rafters, the collar ties would resolve all of these forces.

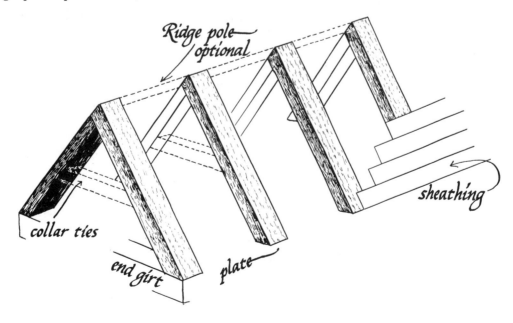

At the ridge, the rafters are actually leaning against each other. Any forces against the roof are dispersed along the rafter portions towards the feet. The steeper the roof pitch, the less push the spreading forces exert at the feet.

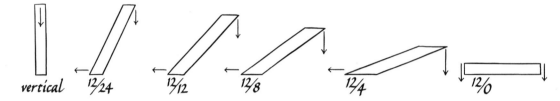

vertical     <sup>12</sup>/24       <sup>12</sup>/12      <sup>12</sup>/8       <sup>12</sup>/4       <sup>12</sup>/0

Another method of resolving the spreading forces is to use a large, vertical timber, called a king post, to support each pair of rafters. Operating in partnership with the king post is the large ridge pole, off which the rafters "hang." Ironically, the use of these timbers tends to reverse the situation — the rafter feet now try to pull together. The tension stabilizes, however, because the feet rest on the plate, so that some of the force is being diverted downward.

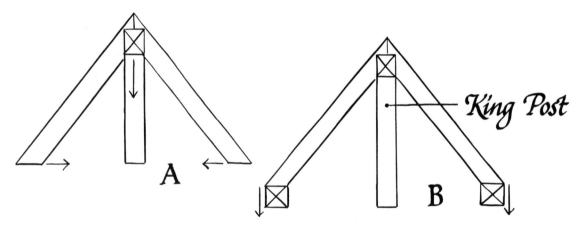

A third option for stabilizing the rafters is to use a major purlin supported by queen posts. This is an old system, one you see used in many a barn today. A queen post meets the rafter at the point at which all the downward pushing forces meet the outward pushing forces. The post actually "captures" the forces at that point and transmits them downward to the posts beneath.

The gambrel roof is a slight variation of this old system. In a gambrel roof, the major purlins are supported by vertical posts, and the roof has two slopes. This system is technically self-supporting. The tendency of the upper set of rafters to spread apart is offset by the major purlins. The purlins are braced in place by the lower rafter set. The rafters, then, form a rigid triangle, with the post supporting the major purlin and with the girt forming the base of the triangle. The rafters in a gambrel roof resemble old buttresses in medieval arches. Braces, collar ties and ridge poles can also be used to provide more rigidity.

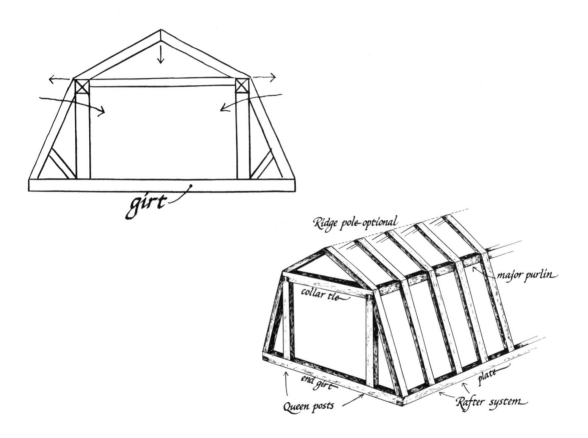

Now that you understand the forces with which rafters contend, you can choose which rafter system you want to use. All of these systems manage to stabilize the forces adequately. Therefore, decide first which direction the joists in the attic floor will lie. If they run from front to back, they will act as the rafter ties. If they run from side to side, you will need an additional system to tie the rafters together. Decide what shape and pitch your roof will be, and whether or not you want an overhang. Then, select the system which best fits your overall plan.

### Principal Rafters and Purlins Roof System

In New England, this is the most common traditional roof system. The rafters are major timbers, 5" x 7" to 7" x 9", placed generally 8 to 12 feet on center. The purlins and ridge pole are small timbers, 3" x 3" to 5" x 5", placed generally 4 feet on center. This system uses the fewest number of rafters. (And since rafters are the most complex timbers to cut and the highest to raise, the fewer the better!) The sheathing boards should be in a vertical position when they are nailed to the rafters. Collar ties set approximately half-way up the rafter are optional, depending on the size of the roof system. Any pitch shallower than a 6/12 is not traditional, and would require special attention.

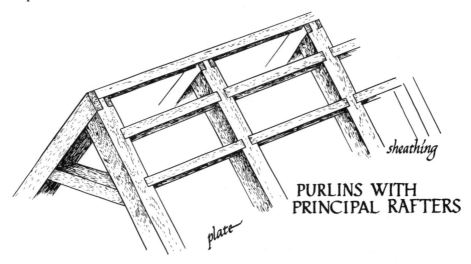

PURLINS WITH
PRINCIPAL RAFTERS

sheathing

plate

### Principal Rafters and Secondary Rafters System

This system was used in barn framing and is less popular in New England. The principal rafters are 6" x 8" to 7" x 9", placed 8 to 12 feet on center. Collar ties are required to stabilize these rafters, and prior to raising, they are assembled, along with the rafters, as a major frame bent. Between these principal rafters lie the secondary rafters, which are 4" x 5" or 4" x 6", and are placed 20 to 30 inches on center. No collar ties are required with secondary rafters, since the main structure is provided by the principal rafters. The main function of the secondary rafters is to provide a nailing surface for the sheathing. Purlins are not necessary if you use this system, and the use of a ridge pole is optional.

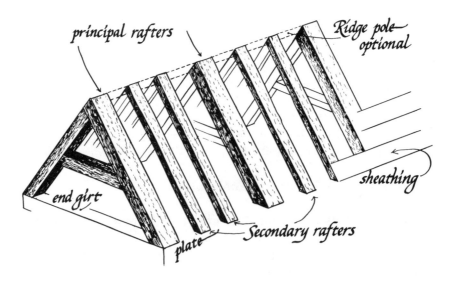

principal rafters

Ridge pole
optional

end girt

plate

Secondary rafters

sheathing

### Principal Rafters Only System

This system is probably as traditional as the principal rafters and purlins system, but it is not commonly found in New England. The rafters are 6'' x 6'' or 7'' x 7'', placed 3 to 4 feet on center. We have seen ridge poles, which are used as often as not in this system, that are as large as the rafters and are supported by a king post. There are no purlins, and collar ties are optional. The sheathing boards should be in a horizontal position when they are nailed to the rafters.

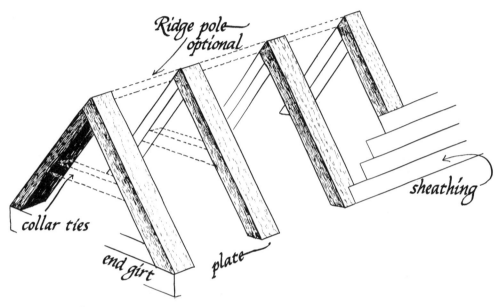

### Options at the Peak

Regardless which of the above systems you use, you have some options as to what method of joining you will use for the rafter pairs at the peak. One choice is to use a mortise and tenon joint, which is the most traditional method, and the method that we use. Another method is to use a half-lap joint. Or, you can half-lap the rafter into a large ridge pole, in which case one member of the rafter pair does not make contact with the other.

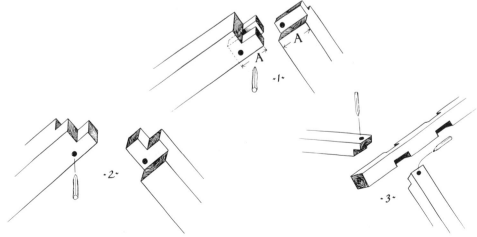

In either of these two systems, the rafters can be boxed decoratively or sized at the ridge.

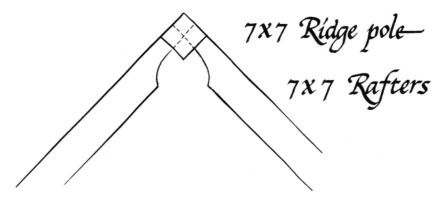

7×7 Ridge pole

7×7 Rafters

## Options at the Foot

There are three traditional joints that can be used at the rafter foot to secure the timber to the plate. Where there is no overhang, we use the birdsmouth joint, which rests on the edge of the plate.

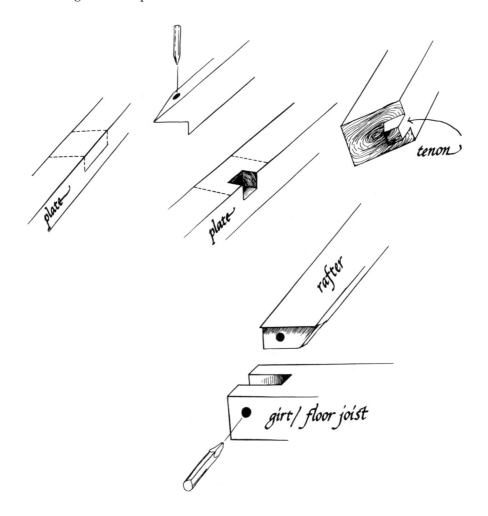

If there is to be an overhang, calculate the dimensions of the overhanging portion of the rafter. You can measure the distance of the total overhang on the rafter, or on the horizontal line.

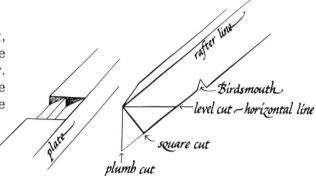

You now know the forces which the rafters must bear, and what your options are for various systems of rafter-making. Once you decide among these systems, you need to know something about the mathematics involved in laying out the rafters.

## ROOF MATHEMATICS

It is important to be careful in calculating your rafter measurements because you will not have a chance to check your accuracy until raising day. Until then, only theory and math can guide you. Yet the rafters must work with each other in a pair, and they also must work with the rest of the frame that you have cut. The first step necessary for laying out rafters is to determine overall length.

There are four different ways to determine rafter length, and, as usual, we have our favorite method. One way to calculate rafter length is to use *Pythagorus's formula.* Any roof can be seen as a collection of right triangles. Two sides of the triangle can be determined from the house dimensions. The third side can be determined using the formula $a^2 + b^2 = c^2$. Let's look at a typical gable roof as an example. One side of the triangle is the rise, or height to the ridge, which we'll call "a." The second known side is the run, which we'll call "b." The hypotenuse, or "c," of the triangle, is the rafter length.

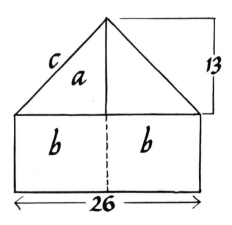

A second method for making these calculations is merely to refer to a table in which a factor has been developed for determining rafter length. If you multiply this factor by the run, you will have the length of the rafter. We are including the table below, but we feel that its use precludes any real understanding of rafters and their relationship to the rest of a structure. The table is useful as a way to double check your own calculations, and it certainly saves time. We would recommend, however, that you use the table only after you have mastered one of the practical methods.

## CONSTANT TABLE FOR COMMON RAFTER LENGTHS WHEN ROOF IS EQUAL PITCH

| Cut | Constant |
|-----|----------|
| 3/12 | 1.03 |
| 4/12 | 1.05 |
| 5/12 | 1.08 |
| 6/12 | 1.12 |
| 7/12 | 1.16 |
| 8/12 | 1.20 |
| 9/12 | 1.25 |
| 10/12 | 1.30 |
| 12/12 | 1.41 |
| 14/12 | 1.54 |
| 15/12 | 1.60 |
| 16/12 | 1.67 |
| 18/12 | 1.80 |
| 20/12 | 1.95 |
| 22/12 | 2.09 |
| 24/12 | 2.24 |
| 26/12 | 2.39 |
| 28/12 | 2.54 |
| 30/12 | 2.70 |
| 32/12 | 2.85 |
| 34/12 | 3.01 |
| 36/12 | 3.17 |
| 38/12 | 3.33 |
| 40/12 | 3.48 |

*Rule to find common rafter length:* Multiply rafter run (one-half the roof span) by the constant given for the required pitch. Result equals rafter length. If roof has a cornice, overhang length must be added to this result. Then increase to a standard length of lumber.

*Example:* If the run is 15 feet and your roof has an 8/12 pitch, multiply 15 times the constant, 1.20, which equals an 18 foot rafter length.

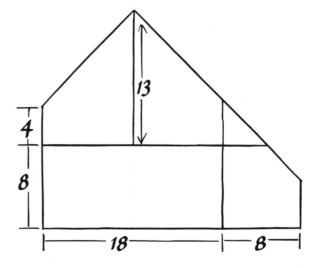

A third method for determining rafter length is called *lofting*. This method requires you to draw your roof on your deck, full scale, and measure the points and angles. This, however, is a very cumbersome way to make calculations. You also would have to delay rafter layout until your first floor frame and deck were cut and laid.

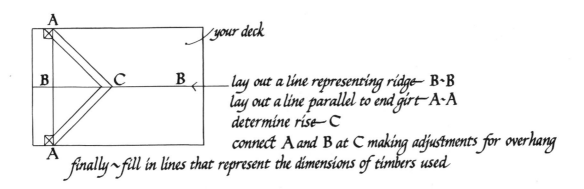

lay out a line representing ridge— B–B
lay out a line parallel to end girt—A–A
determine rise—C
connect A and B at C making adjustments for overhang
finally~fill in lines that represent the dimensions of timbers used

A fourth method, which we've saved for last, is the most difficult to master, yet it is the method which best helps the builder to understand rafters. It requires the use and understanding of an invaluable tool, the *framing square*. While whole books have been written about the use of this one tool, we will try to give you enough information here for you to be able to use it. Meanwhile, please read *Roof Framing* by H. H. Siegele.

The framing square has a 24 inch blade, called the body, and a 16 inch arm, called the tongue. Please also purchase two points, which are moveable buttons or knobs which can be set and tightened anywhere along the body or tongue. Think of this tool as a miniature roof system, with the body representing the run, and the tongue representing the rise. By setting the points to a given roof pitch, the rise and run can be kept constant for determining rafter lengths. Remember that the roof pitch is expressed as a ratio. For example, a 9/12 pitch means that for every 9 inches that the roof slope rises vertically, it measures 12 inches on the horizontal.

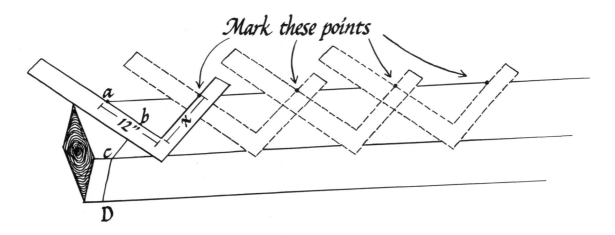

There are some advantages to expressing the roof pitch as some number "in twelve." The number twelve happens to be in the middle of the body of the framing square and allows for some flexibility in measuring in both directions. Secondly, building measurements are usually expressed in feet. Therefore, the measuring base is kept consistent for the rafters and the other components of the frame.

By setting the square points and keeping the rise and run constant you will be able to determine the rafter length with a process called *stepping off*. To describe this process, let's try to determine the length of a rafter for a roof with a 9/12 pitch. Set the point on the body of the framing square at twelve and the point on the tongue at nine. To "step off" the rafter length, move the square along the rafter on the top surface, marking the necessary intersections, as shown in the drawing. When using a ratio to step off the roof, the number of times that you move the square will always be the same number that describes the run of your building. For example, a 26 foot wide building would have a 13 foot run, and you would step off the rafter 13 times.

We prefer to set the square points to the actual rise and run of the building. For example, if the rise were 13 feet and the run were 15 feet, the points would be so set on the tongue and body respectively. Measuring the distance between 13 and 15 feet gives you the rafter length. When using the actual building dimensions to step off the rafter length, you always move the square along the rafter 12 times. You do this because you have made with the framing square a miniature-scale roof system in inches which you are now blowing back up to full scale in feet by stepping off twelve times. This method helps to eliminate errors because you are using actual building information, not a ratio, formula, table, or conversion.

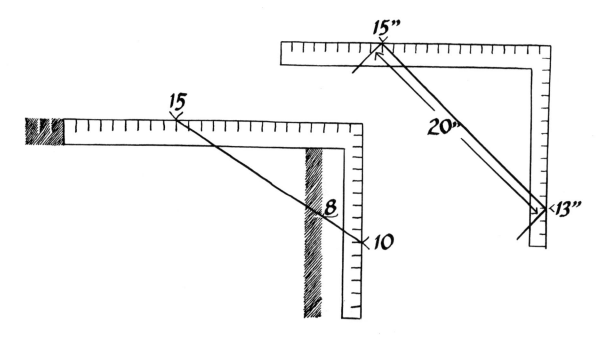

The specifics for using this method will be presented in the next section on laying out and cutting rafters. For now, we wanted to familiarize you with the framing square and the method. Decide which combination of methods best suits your needs.

## LAYING OUT PRINCIPAL RAFTERS AND PURLINS ROOF SYSTEM

### Overall Length

The first step in laying out the rafters is to determine the overall length. The male rafters will be shorter than the female rafters by some 4 inches. If you have some rafter sticks that are short for some reason, you can use them as male rafters.

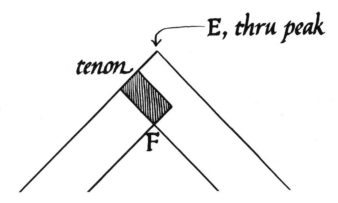

We find it is useful to lay out both the male and female measurements on one timber. Except for the joinery at the peak, all the male and female rafters will be the same. Therefore, once you have stepped off one rafter in this manner and checked it, you have determined the length of the remaining male and female rafters. You then need only a bevel square and those measurements to lay out the remaining rafters.

Set your points by using one of the two methods described in the previous section. Starting at point "a" on the timber, step off the necessary number of times, marking the points as in the drawing below.

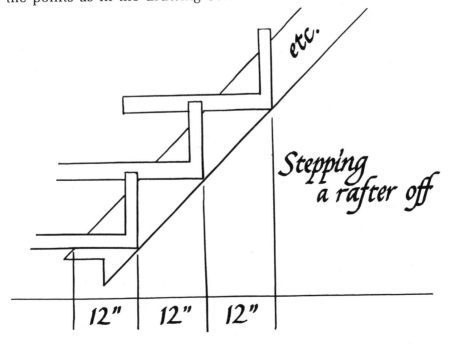

The last mark is the peak. Mark points E and F (which will represent a plumb line).

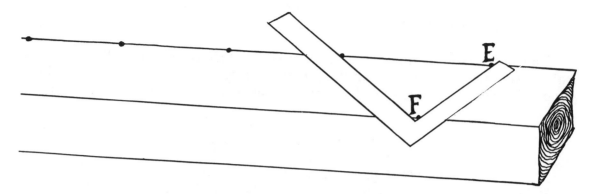

Turn the square over and hold it on point E at the number that describes the width of the timber, and at point F where the square touches this point. Mark out line F-G. With the straight edge of the square, join points F and H with a line. Any inaccuracies would be multiplied when you extend the line to point H. Also, this line is cut and will be exposed on the male rafter.

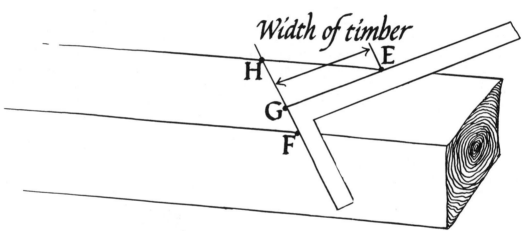

Next, draw a line parallel to F-H starting at point E and extending to point J. Use the bevel square to do this, being very careful not to vary line F-H. With these four points established, draw the square lines down the edges of the timber and connect them on the back side.

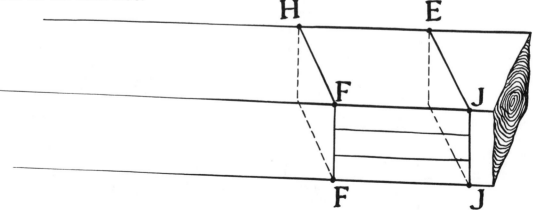

When you cut the rafters, E-J is the cut-off line for the female, and H-F represents the shoulder of the tenon on the male rafter.

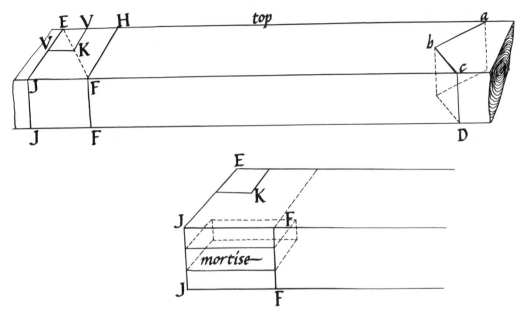

### The Peak

To lay out the tenon for the male rafter, mark lines between F-F and J-J to represent the thickness of the tenon. The length of the tenon — 4 inches or so — is measured using line H-F as a reference point. This same section also delineates the area of the mortise for the female rafter. Use F-J as a reference point, and measure the 4 inches or so depth down line H-F.

### Purlin Layout

If your roof system is using purlins, mark them out using point E as your reference point. Lay out the desired centers for the purlin pockets. We use 4 foot centers and 4" x 4" purlins. Note that these marks are square to the *timber*, regardless of roof pitch.

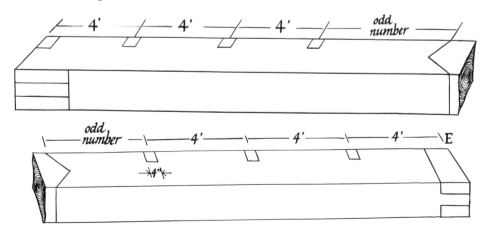

The purlins will either be square-cut or haunched half-laps. It is important during the layout to make note of which rafters will be used at the gable ends. On these rafters, the pockets for the purlins are only laid out on the *inside* surfaces. On all the other rafters, the pockets can be transposed to the other side of each rafter by laying the square across the top of the timber and marking the points. Use a combination square and mark out the mortises as before.

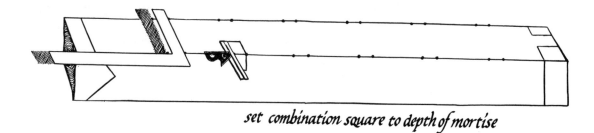

*set combination square to depth of mortise*

### Foot Layout

To lay out a birdsmouth, mark the horizontal line which will rest on the plate by using the framing square with the points set. From point a, measure to point b the distance equal to the thickness of the plate.

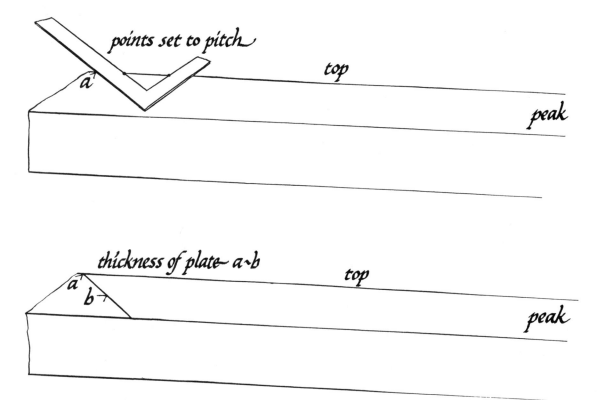

Lay out the plumb line from point b to the edge of the timber. Then, turn the square over so that the tongue is in your left hand and the points are on the bottom surface. You can disregard the points and set the square on the line. Then draw the square line, b-c.

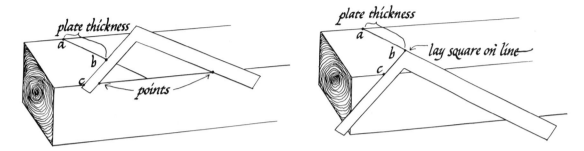

The next step is to carry these lines out to the other side of the rafter to assure clean, square cuts. It is especially important to do this if you plan to use a circular saw. Set a square on edge at point c and lay out the square line, c-D, and a-D on the top and bottom surfaces of the rafter. Finally, complete the birdsmouth on the other side to match the completed side. Use the two points D as a reference point.

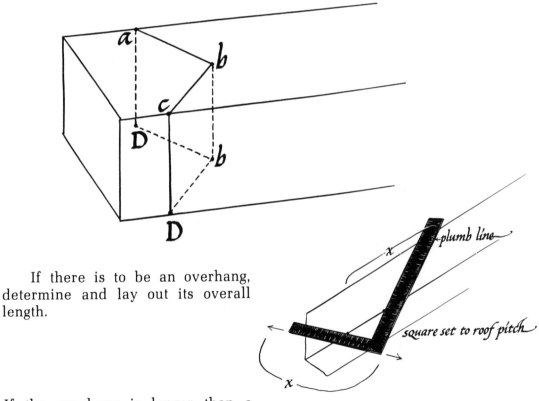

If there is to be an overhang, determine and lay out its overall length.

If the overhang is longer than a dimension on the square, simply step off as you did for the rafter.

After this point is established, the cuts can be plumb, square, horizontal, or any combination of these.

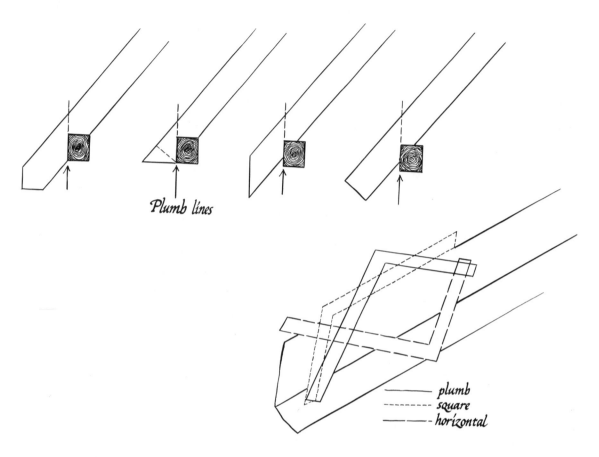

Plumb lines

—— plumb
- - - square
— - — horizontal

Next, decide on the birdsmouth and its relationship to the plate. Use the plumb line that represents the outside of the plate as a reference point. As you can see, there are quite a few choices. As usual, we like the traditional solution, that of using a sizable joint on the rafter and plate to resolve the lift and spreading forces the joint will bear. Lay out the thickness of the plate from the plumb line.

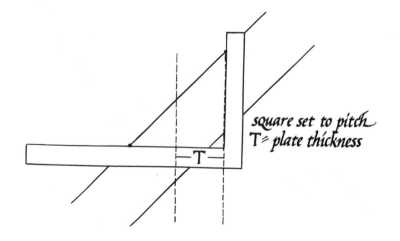

square set to pitch
T = plate thickness

Next, lay out a horizontal line to represent the top of the plate where this line intersects the bottom of the rafter.

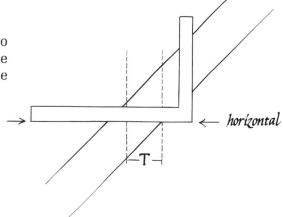

Half-way along the horizontal line, lay out a third plumb line. This represents the shoulder of the mouth.

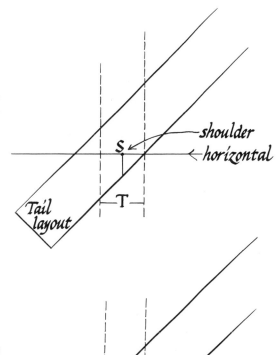

Now you have two choices on how to proceed from point S. One is to lay out a line parallel to the top of the rafter towards the tail cut. The second is to lay out a horizontal line to the tail. The first method is more commonly used.

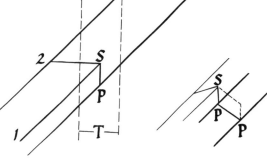

This first method also requires that, in making the mortise, you make saw kerfs and do some chisel work to relieve the outside of the plate.

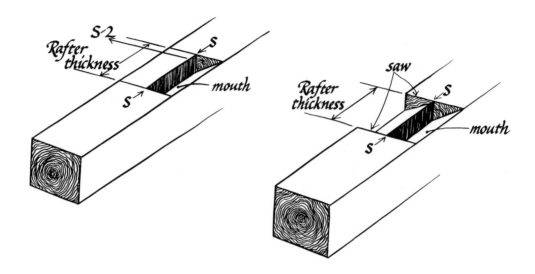

For the second method, you need only a chisel to make the mortise.

Along with the birdsmouth and the overhang methods, you can also lay out at the foot using a tenon. Follow the rules for laying out a full-width tenon, with these exceptions. The horizontal cut of the rafter will be the shoulder of the tenon. Also, the end of the tenon will have to be level cut. This is necessary so that the tenon does not protrude beyond the width of the building. The mortise is laid out to match the tenon.

### Ridge Pole Pocket Layout

If you have decided to use a ridge pole, set the heel of the square to point K so that the tongue and body of the square intersect the top edge of the timber and the end of the timber, respectively. The distance between points V and K will equal the dimensions of the ridge pole.

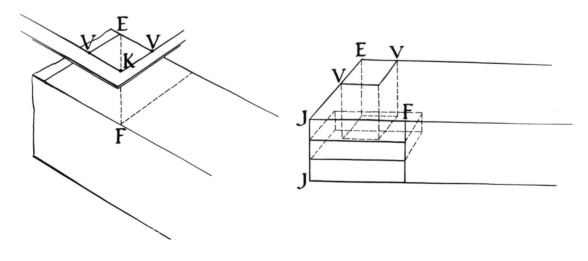

When you lay out the ridge pole for a roof system with a pitch that is other than square, the top two surfaces must be cut to match the roof pitch.

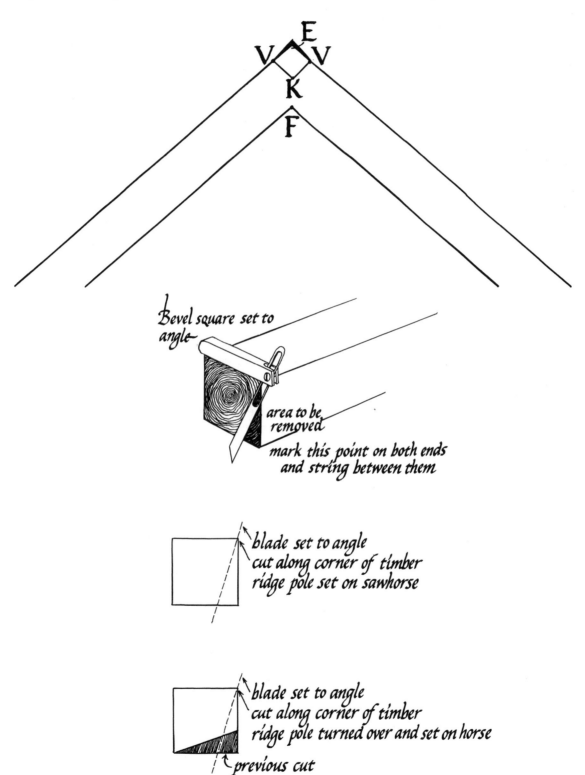

Bevel square set to angle

area to be removed

mark this point on both ends and string between them

blade set to angle
cut along corner of timber
ridge pole set on sawhorse

blade set to angle
cut along corner of timber
ridge pole turned over and set on horse

previous cut

### Variations

If you choose to use a half-lap joint at the peak, you must make an adjustment in the tenon on the male rafter. Instead of centering the tenon and making it shorter, you will lay it out full length on one side of the rafter. Lay out lines to represent the cut-off lines. On one side of the rafter, H-F is the cut-off line and shoulder. On the other side, E-J is the cut-off line.

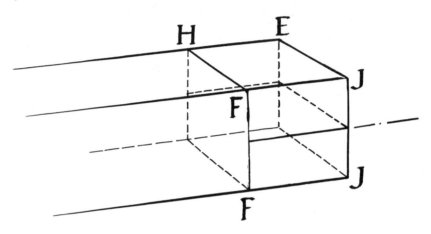

With the half-lap joint, you will use smaller stock for the rafters, and place them on closer centers. You will most likely not use purlins or a ridge pole. If you do, you will have to lay out on the male rafter as well as on the female rafter for the ridge pole pocket. Purlins will be laid out as we described above. Lay out the female rafter as you would any half-lap joint. Remember to match the male to the female, keeping all angles and the layout for the ridge in mind.

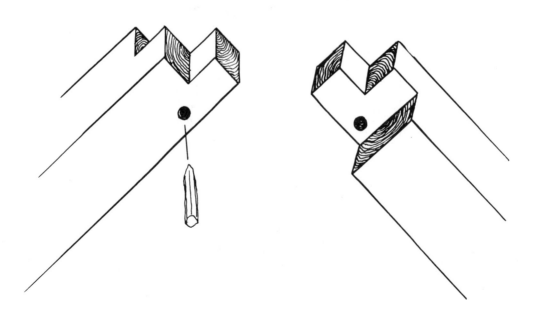

If you choose to half-lap into a large ridge pole, you will use a somewhat different layout. The overall length of the rafter will be determined by adding on the length of the lap, but subtracting the dimension of the ridge pole.

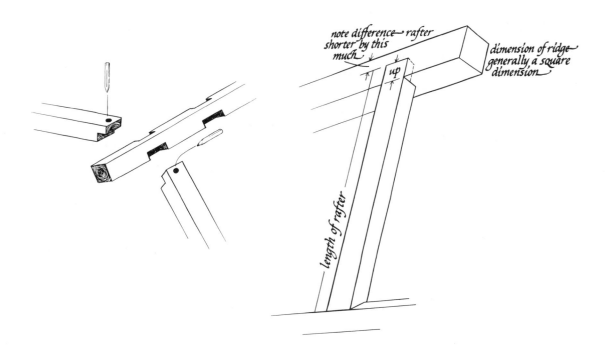

Step off the length as before, and lay out the dimensions of the ridge pole and the lap.

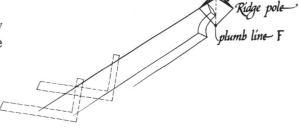

If you have already altered the ridge pole to correspond to the roof, then you can find the rafter pocket dimensions by just measuring the ridge pole. Otherwise, lay a straight edge on line E-F. Then lay the framing square on this line as you did before when you laid out the ridge pole.

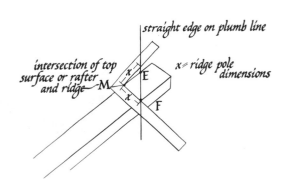

From point M, measure the length of
the lap in the direction of the peak.
Lay out the lap as usual, remember-
ing to consider the angles. Because of
its angles, a standard half-lap will
require quite a bit of fudging during
raising. The old-timers skirted this
difficulty by removing the shoulder
to some pleasing point and calling
the result a "dressed shoulder."

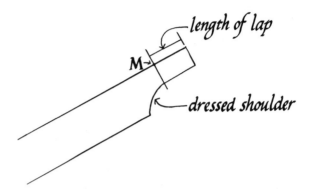

The layout is simplified if the roof pitch is square. In this case, the lap can be
left square and the ridge pole will not require any angle cuts on the top surface. In
this system, the rafters and ridge are generally square timbers to begin with, that
is, 5" x 5", 6" x 6" or 7" x 7".

The last special situation we will explain is that of laying out dormer rafters.
We do not use dormers very often because they are not part of the original timber-
frame tradition in New England. Dormers were almost always added on years after
the house was raised. However, if you want the extra space and light that dormers
afford, we will explain how to lay out the lines. First, mark on a wide board the
pitch of the dormer rafter, such as 4/12. Draw line a-b to represent the horizontal
cut of the dormer rafter.

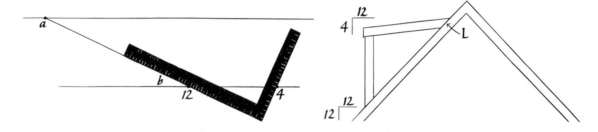

Next, set your square on this line to the pitch of the main roof, such as 12/12.
This may have to be reduced in order to fit within the length of line a-b. Hold points
C-D on line a-b, and read points E-F. Set these points on the square. This ratio,
represented by line L on the blade of the square, is the angle of the cut of the
dormer roof *only* where it meets the main roof.

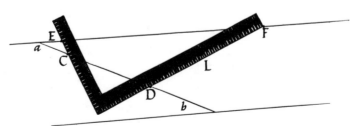

*points C & D = ¹²⁄₁₂ or any convenient ratio that will fit
within line a-b ~ ¹⁰⁄₁₀  ⁶⁄₆ etc.*

All other dormer rafter layouts are made from the original roof pitch. Any dormer pitch can be used on any main roof pitch, and this pitch can be found in the same manner.

## CUTTING RAFTER JOINTS

The cutting of rafter joints differs only slightly from general cutting rules. You must remember that unless your pitch is square, the shoulders will not be square to the timber. Relieving the waste for the ridge pole pocket on the female is a matter of sawing out the small block of wood. Then bore and chisel out the mortises as usual. To cut the proper angles on the ridge pole for other than a 12/12 pitch, set the circular saw blade to the proper angle of the roof. Most saws will not saw all the way through. The expanse that the saw won't reach can be chopped out with a broad hatchet. You can use a broad axe or hatchet to do the whole ridge. Simply strike chalk lines on the face of the timber and remove wood to that line.

Once you have mastered the framing square and have cut your first complete rafter system, you will certainly have cause for celebration.

# 10 TRADITIONAL DECORATIVE TREATMENTS OF TIMBERS

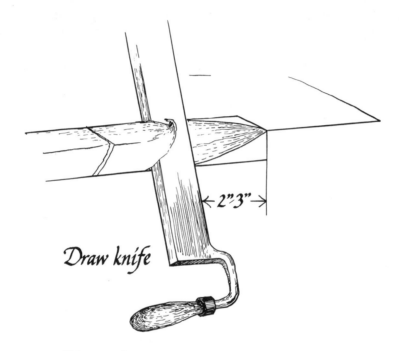

In this chapter, we will be explaining how to square a log, how to cut gunstock posts, and how to champher and bead the timbers. The early builders had no choice about the squaring of their own timbers. All the timbers had to be molded into some useable form for timbers, studs, boards and miscellaneous framing sticks. Even if the early timber framers were building a log cabin, they made certain surfaces level so that a floor board or sheathing board would lie flat on them. Often, they kept these cuts to a minimum by having a dirt floor with no framing.

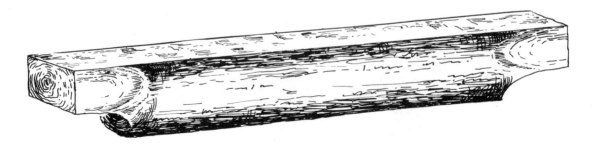

Some of you may want to square your logs by hand, even though the existence of power mills gives us the choice not to. You will need four to six different kinds of broad axes and adzes if you plan to square your own logs. This is how it is done.

### Squaring Logs

The cutting process is the same whether you are squaring one surface or four. First, make "cribs" or holding logs by notching out a place on two short butts of logs which will cradle the log being cut.

Once the log to be cut is in place in the cribs, mark out on the end of the log the desired size of the finished timber. Keep the lines square. Then draw or score lines the length of the log from each corner to its opposing corner.

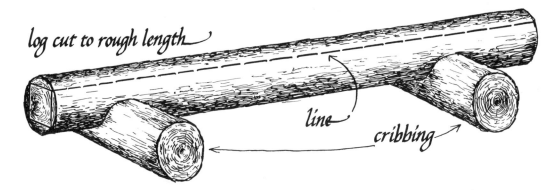

*log cut to rough length*

*line*

*cribbing*

Next, "score" or chop the area between the two top lines with a single-bit or double-bit axe. These cuts should be only as deep as necessary to reach the desired timber size.

Use a heavy broad axe to remove the bulk of the wood. Try doing this with the log on its side to see if it is an easier way for you to work.

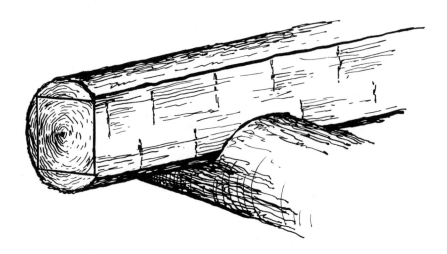

The last step is to adze all the surfaces smooth. The surface you are working on in this phase should be on top.

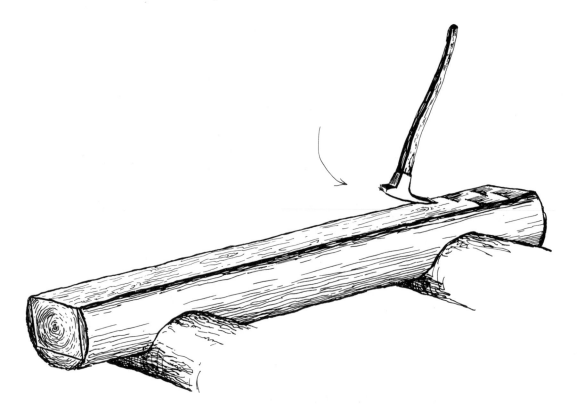

Simply repeat this process for your timbers, making sure that you lay out properly for the various timber sizes in your frame. You can hand plane as a final step if you want an even smoother timber surface.

### Gunstocks

A gunstock post is structurally functional. It offers full bearing for all the timbers that come together on it. Like a haunch, it becomes a shoulder for the timbers to rest on. Therefore, it could quite simply be a post having extra width at the top. However, the craftsmen who created the early timber frames wanted the posts to be not only functional, but also to be handsome. Therefore, you can choose among several decorative options for these hard-working posts, and again, you can either use hand tools or power tools to make them.

A gunstock post is 2 to 4 inches wider at the top than it is at the bottom. It usually is milled as a square timber equal to the thickness of the plates and girts it will be supporting. For example, if the plates and girts are 7" x 9"s, the post would be a 7" x 9" or a 7" x 11". The simplest solution is to taper the post. If one chooses to cut a gunstock shape, you can choose a simple one or a more elaborate one.

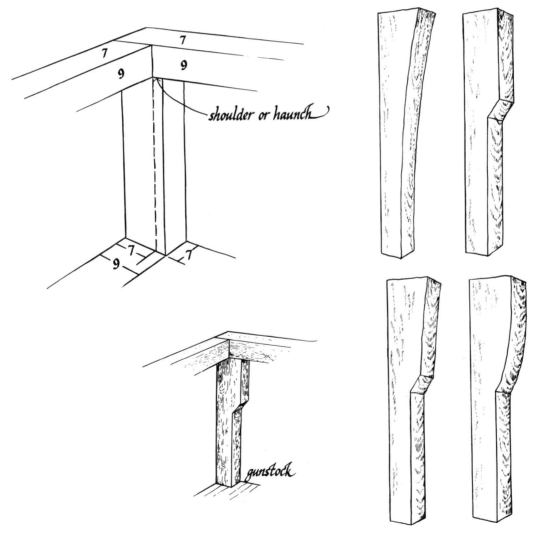

Some other varieties of gunstocks

A tapered post is 2 to 4 inches wider at the top than at the bottom. Lay the post on its back with the end being tapered on top. Strike a chalk line from the top of the timber to the bottom. Make axe kerfs close to this line.

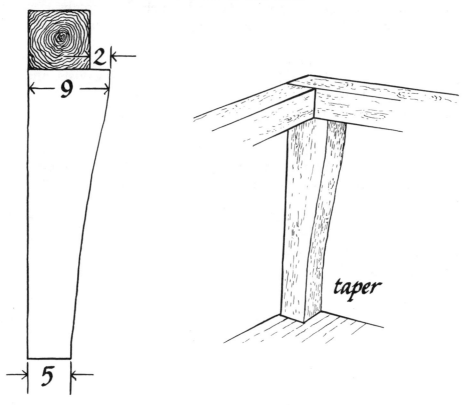

Adze down the post starting at the top so that you are working with the grain of the wood. Otherwise, you risk splitting into the body of the post. If you encounter a knot, you will have to come in from both directions at that point.

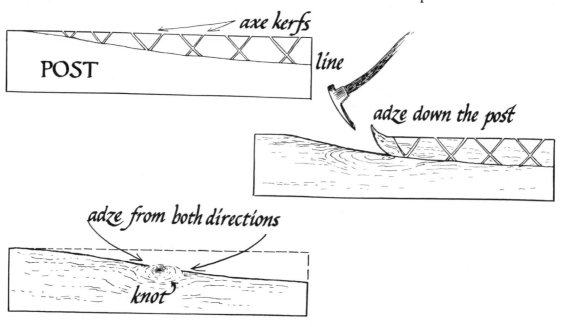

The gunstock detail on the post is so called because that is what it resembles. The length of the shoulder part of the post is about 25 inches. The narrower section of the post is 2 to 3 inches smaller than the shoulder width.

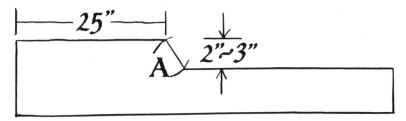

The transition between the shoulder and the narrower section can be resolved in several ways.

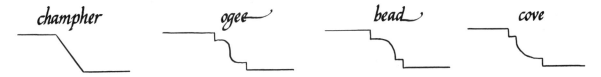

It is difficult to cut these, and the proper tools are required. First, hand cut your decoration for the area of transition.

You can use a piece of heavy cardboard, masonite, or even a 3/4 inch board to make up a template, or pattern, for the detail. Draw the pattern full scale, including the top wide part of the timber, and a portion of the narrower section. Transfer the pattern to both sides of the timber. Then, use hand tools to carefully carve out the design.

Strike a straight line from the detail to the bottom of the post and then make cuts with an axe or chain saw to this line.

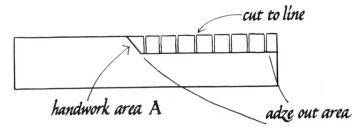

If power is available, you can make the long rip from the bottom of the timber to the gunstock detail with a power circular saw. You will then still have to use an adze to cut away the area, unless your saw is a 10 or 12 inch one, or unless your posts are unusually small. It is also possible to rip the entire post with a timber hand saw, which is much like the old pit saw. This, however, would be tedious work.

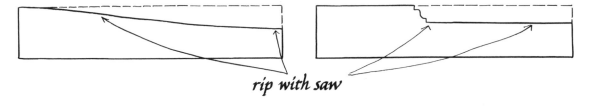

## Champhers and Beads

Champhers and beads are purely decorative. This kind of decorative detail was very important to the old craftsmen because their work was exposed. In the old days, the extent to which a structure was ornamented depended on the skill, time, and money available. Therefore, there was an order of priority as to which timbers would be decorated. The summer would come first, and then, if the resources were still available, the posts, then the girts and plates.

These details should be cut before the timbers are raised. Molding planes of various sizes are used to cut the beads, and a draw knife is used to cut the champhers. As with all detail work, champhers can be simple or elaborate depending on your skill and taste.

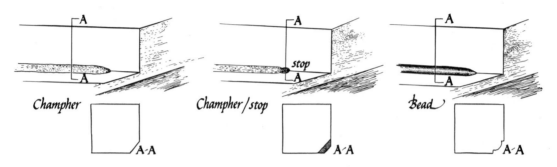

The bead and champher end with a decorative cut called a "stop." First, decide where on the timber you would like these stops to be. We generally stop our champhers and beads some 6 to 8 inches from the exposed ends of the timber. Strike two chalk lines from one stop point to the other on the corner surfaces to outline the champher. Keep in mind how wide the champher will be as well. We usually make ours 2 inches wide.

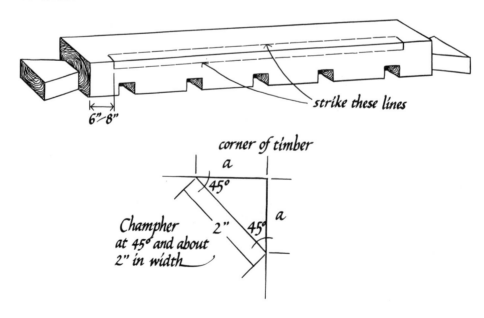

Use a hatchet or a chisel and carefully cut out close to the lines as much of the waste as you can. At the ends you will have to make shallower cuts because the stop will taper up to the corner surface of the timber.

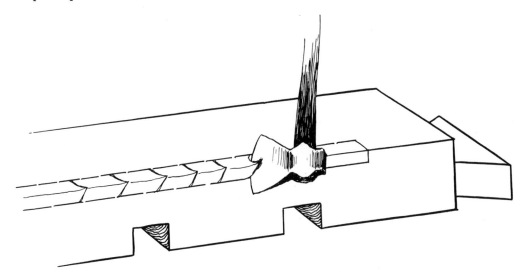

Next, use a draw knife to cut in gradually at the stop. Draw the knife for a distance of 2 to 3 inches before you reach the full depth of the champher.

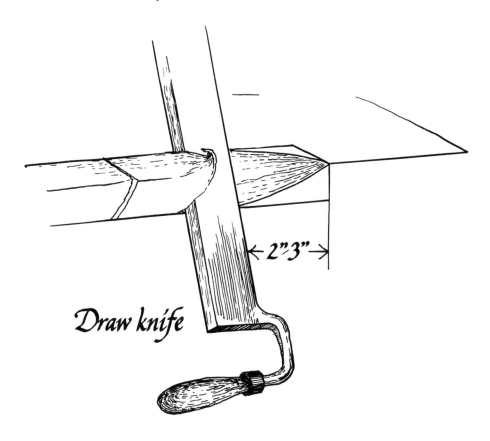

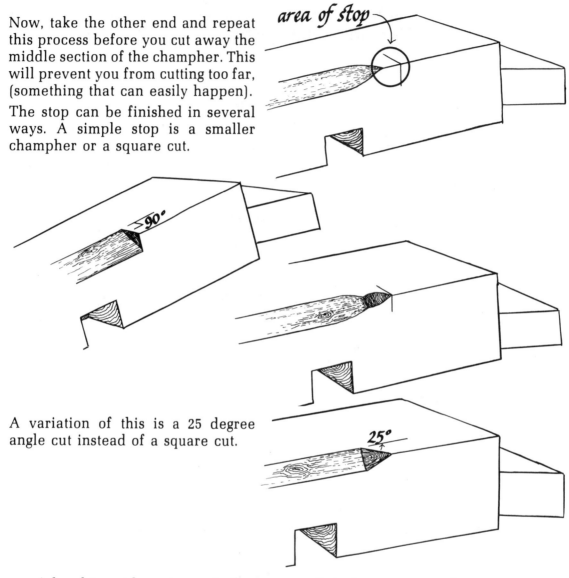

Now, take the other end and repeat this process before you cut away the middle section of the champher. This will prevent you from cutting too far, (something that can easily happen).

The stop can be finished in several ways. A simple stop is a smaller champher or a square cut.

*area of stop*

*90°*

A variation of this is a 25 degree angle cut instead of a square cut.

*25°*

A bead is cut by using a similar process. It is, however, simpler to cut a bead because it is not necessary to strike the chalk lines. The molding plane will do this for you. You will not be able to taper up to the top surface at the stops as you did with the draw knife because the head of the plane will prevent you from getting that close. Therefore, there is a little more handwork involved in cutting a bead.

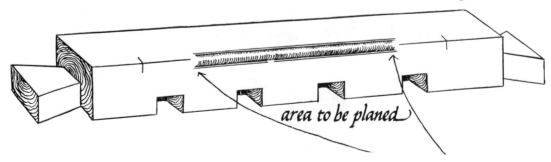

*area to be planed*

To cut the stops for the bead, you will first need to round out a portion of the bead by hand. Then, make square cuts to meet the bead.

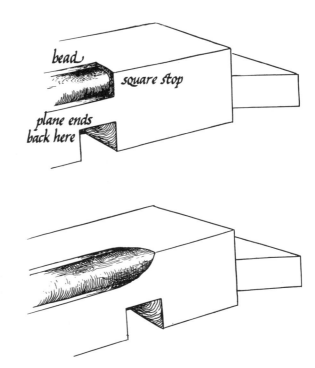

It is simpler to round out a portion of the bead by hand and then let it meet the top surface without the square cuts.

Here is an illustration of how the decorated timbers will look once they are assembled. Note the relationship between the undecorated portion of the summer and the undecorated portion of the girt. Likewise, note the relationship of the undecorated portions of girt and plate and the shoulder of the gunstock post.

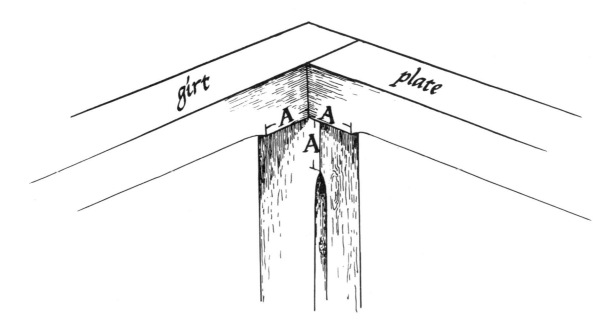

# 11 RAISIN' DAY

The process of raising a frame is simple if you are organized. Therefore, we begin this chapter with some suggestions on organization techniques, tools, and procedures. If your preparations for raising are thorough, the mechanics are easily mastered.

## ORGANIZATION

### Backfilling

Prior to raising, arrange to have the area around your foundation backfilled. This means having someone come in with a bulldozer to push back the dirt around the foundation walls. If this isn't done, you will be carrying both yourself and heavy timbers across a ditch, a dangerous and difficult procedure. Before you raise the frame, your foundation should have at least ten days to set after it is poured or built. Twenty-eight days is ideal.

### Electrical Power

If you do not already have electrical power at the site, and you intend to use it, you should have an electrician set up a temporary service box on a tree near the site. Then, call your electric company and ask them to hook up the temporary service. Or, you might prefer to use a generator.

### Checking the Measurements

Be sure you have checked the measurements of both your foundation and all the timbers and joints you have cut. Be sure to correct any oversized portions of any of the joints by boxing the timbers. (It is time-consuming, and discouraging, to find major discrepancies on raising day.)

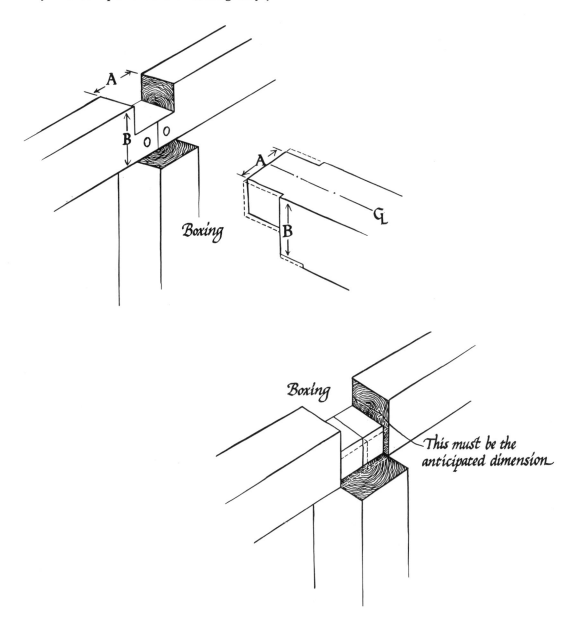

### Organizing Timbers

Organize the timbers at the site so that they are located near the place in the house where they will be raised. Also, try to store them facing the same general direction that they'll be eventually when they are positioned in the frame.

## TOOLS AND EQUIPMENT

These are the basic tools you should have on hand:

> a minimum of three 50 foot pieces of rope
> a block and tackle
> a come along
> two or more beetles and sledges
> wedges, drills and augers
> pegs (trenails)
> chisels, mallets, levels, hammers, planes, saws
> measuring devices, plumb bob
> two 8 foot step ladders, two 8 foot ladders, one 16 foot ladder.

### Temporary Braces

You will also need stock for temporary braces. These are 1" x 6" boards ranging in length from 8 to 16 feet.

### Shims

Have some wood shingles to use as shims for adjusting the timbers to make them level.

### Staging

Staging equipment is necessary when you raise girts and plates. We use butt ends of timbers accumulated during joint cutting to step on or to support planks. Have some 8 and 10 foot ladders available.

### Manpower

Several kinds of manpower are necessary. You'll need people to help with the raising, someone to chop the pine bough that will go atop the ridge, someone to organize the beverages, and someone to organize the food.

## GENERAL PROCEDURES

There are some things you should check several times during the raising process.

### Checking for Square

It is very important to check for square frequently. You do this by measuring diagonal points.

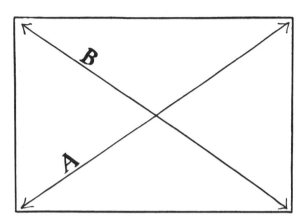

diagonal **A** ≠ diagonal **B**

### Checking for Level

You also must check for level. This is especially critical when you are checking the measurements of your foundation, and when you have laid the sills. The most accurate way of doing this is to mount a level on a tripod. You probably will need to rent a level for siting the high and low points of your foundation, so arrange to rent it again on raising day. Have someone stand beside the foundation. They should be holding a long stick, steel retractable rule, or preferably, a wooden folding rule. Looking through the level, note a measurement or point c, and then have the other person stand at other points about 10 feet apart. The existence of any points higher on the rule than the original point c indicates that the framing is too low. Any point lower than point c means the frame is too high. Choose the lowest point in relation to point c and, using wood shingles, shim the rest of the frame (the sills and chimney girts) until all points are consistently even with the highest point.

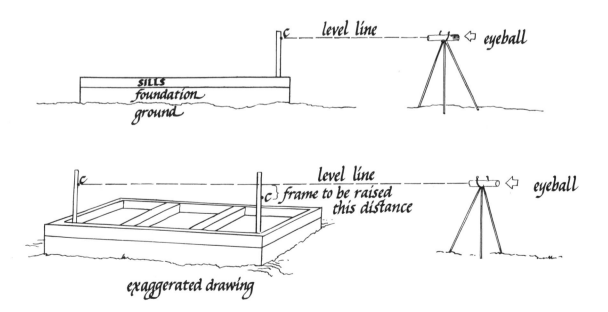

exaggerated drawing

### Checking for Straight Lines

One way to check for straight lines is to look down the line of the sills for any concave or convex lines. If your frame has additions or ells, you may not be able to do this. In that case, you may tack 1 inch blocks at the corners of the sills. Pull a piece of string tightly over the blocks and wind the string securely around a nail at either end of the sill. Then use a piece of wood the same thickness as the blocks, inserting it between the string and the sill along the sill from corner to corner. You should note any variations in the distance between string and frame since this would indicate that the lines of the timbers are not straight.

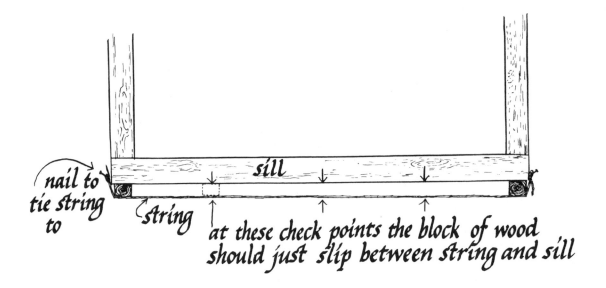

*nail to tie string to*  *string*  *sill*  *at these check points the block of wood should just slip between string and sill*

### Checking for Plumb

This should also become a habit. Hold a 4 foot level vertically against the timbers to be sure they are not standing or lying at an angle, but are straight up and down. Or more accurately, use a plumb bob much like the 1 inch blocks and string by holding the line 1 inch away from the top of a post and making sure the point of the plumb is 1 inch away from the base.

### Lifting

We want to remind you again about the proper method for lifting. Remember to use your legs, not your back, and always have enough people to do the job. A 6" x 12" timber 16 feet long weighs approximately 350 to 450 pounds, depending on its degree of dryness and its species. A board foot of wood weighs about 4 to 6 pounds.

### Laying Decks

When laying decking, remember to stagger the ends of the boards so that they do not all end on a particular joist in succession.

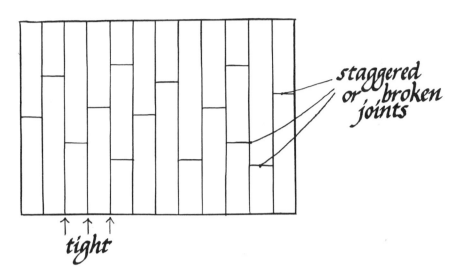

Make sure the boards are tight against each other and that they are straight and consistent with the perimeter lines. Pay special attention as you cut the mortises through the decking to receive the tenons on the posts. Be careful that you do not hit any concealed decking nails with your chisels or bits as these will be damaged extensively and the raising will be delayed.

### Temporary Bracing

Temporary bracing has two functions. First of all, it holds a post or group of timbers in place until the joining timbers are also raised. It also holds the frame in a square, level, and plumb position until the permanent braces are put in. In both cases, it is important to position the braces so that they provide maximum support but do not interfere with the raising process. It will mean a duplication of effort if temporary braces have to be removed in order for you to put in the purlins or the permanent braces. So, a little forethought is advisable. Generally, it is a good idea to tack the 1" x 6" board as high up as possible on the stick or bent being braced, and bring it down at a 45 degree angle to the sill or plate.

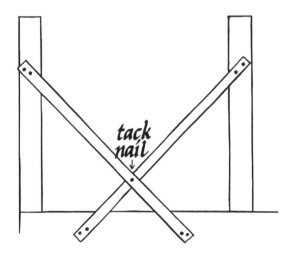

Use several 8d or 10d nails only partially nailed in so that they will be easily retractable. Cross brace by laying a brace across the first in the opposite direction. Tack these two together at the point where they cross. When you brace a rafter pair, tack the board to the *underside* of the rafter, again as high up as possible, and bring it down at a 45 degree angle to the plate. Now you will not have to remove the bracing to set the purlins.

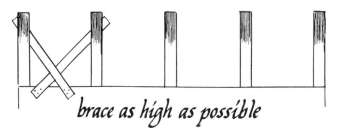

*brace as high as possible*

## THE RAISING PROCESS

### First Floor Frame

We will begin with the sills and chimney girts for the first floor frame. These are simply set in their logical places, matching joints. Check for square, level, plumb, and straight lines.

Next, lay the joists crown up. Any framing for the masonry or stairs to a cellar should be done at this time.

Next, if you are laying the decks as part of the frame raising, lay the first floor deck, leaving open the spaces for masonry and stairs. This completes the first floor frame.

### Second Floor Frame

There are two methods for raising the rest of the frame. One is to build a bent on the deck and raise it as a unit. Traditionally, there would usually be four bents. The other is to raise each stick, one at a time, bracing it until the joining sticks are in place. Generally, we use the second method and would recommend it for novice raisers. Individual timbers are lighter than bents, and therefore, require a smaller work force. Also, there are fewer details to think about at one time. This method does take a long time. In either method, the first step would be to cut all the necessary mortises for the posts. Check the measurements and their positions.

If you are raising a bent, carry the necessary posts and girts for one bent onto the deck, and lay them out with the tenons at their respective mortises.

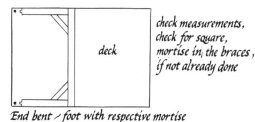

*deck*

*check measurements,*
*check for square,*
*mortise in the braces,*
*if not already done*

*End bent / foot with respective mortise*

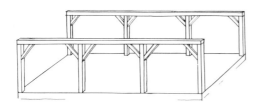 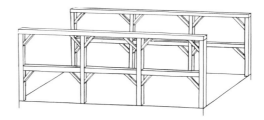

You will need a few categories of workers for the raising. You need people at the girt to lift, people at the mortises to guide the posts in, people to check for plumb, and people to nail the temporary braces. If the house is a single story, the workers will always be able to reach and support the girt once it is in position. However, if the house is one-and-a-half or more stories, an additional group of workers are needed to use barn poles, or pikes, to help lift the bent once it is too high to reach by hand.

Remember that at the beginning stages of lifting the bent, the feet of the posts will tend to move out more than down. When the bent is almost upright, and there is more weight pushing down, the tenons will then tend to move downward into the mortises more than outward.

The pikes should be set as soon as the upper framing is lifted to head height. Additional pikes can be set as the bent gets higher.

"All together girls ... Hup"

start barn pikes here

add more pikes as bent is raised

note : lines are made to the bent to prevent from going too far over

The pressure applied by all the people raising must be consistent along the entire line of the bent. Timing and rhythm are very important. Therefore, one person among the group should be a caller. This is someone who sets the lifting rhythm and audibly guides the raising with "easy," "all together now," "hupp!" or whatever suits the situation.

Tie ropes to the girts prior to raising the bent. People in your crew should hold these ropes in order to prevent the bent from going over too far.

With the first bent in place, lay out the second bent in the same way. If the first bent is very securely braced, you can use a block and tackle with it to help raise the second bent. The second can be used similarly for the third, and so on.

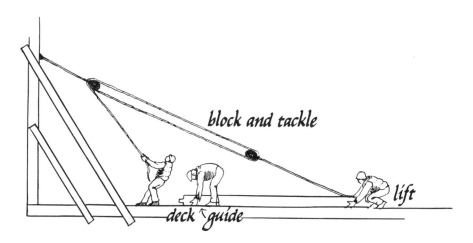

After the second bent is in place and braced, raise the front and rear plates for that section to tie the two bents together. The process of setting these major timbers will require undoing the temporary bracing. The plates are generally slid in from the side by spreading the two bents apart. This process requires some careful planning. Have one set of people hold the plate at the proper elevation while another group unnails the braces and spreads the bents apart a few inches.

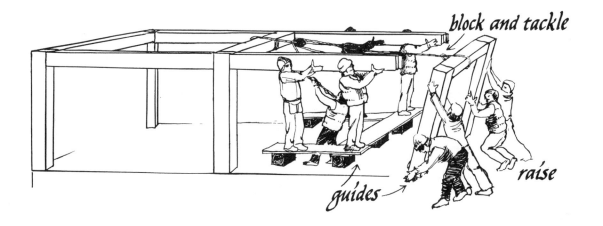

Once the plate is in place, use a come along to apply a great deal of pressure to pull the posts toward each other.

*come along ⁄ to apply a great deal of pressure on pulling the posts toward each other*

Once the joints look very tight, bore the necessary holes for the trenails and insert them.

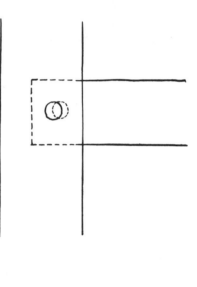

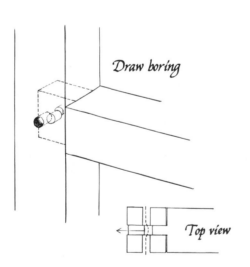

*Draw boring*

*Top view*

Follow the same procedure for the rear plate.

Because the dovetail joint is not flexible enough to allow for the setting of the plates after the summer, the summer timber, if there is to be one, is the last major timber raised in this section. Raise the summer and lay it upside down on the girts. Then, roll the timber over and set the tenons into the mortises. The dovetail joint will fit tightly, and a beetle is usually required to whomp it down into the pockets. Prior to fitting the dovetail joint, set two temporary posts, one under each girt at the mortise of the summer. These will provide some support and prevent the timber from bouncing as you are hammering it with the beetle.

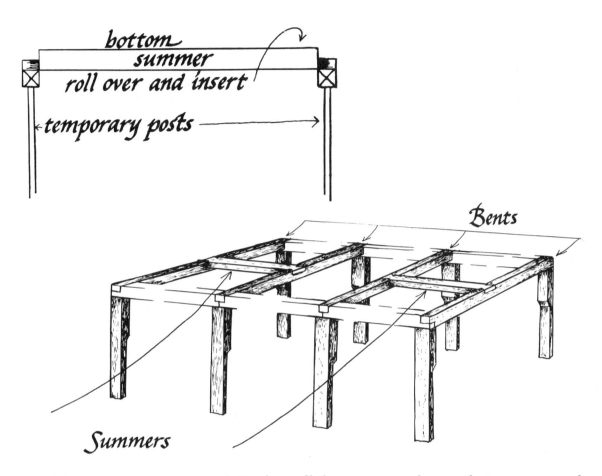

The summer is not pegged. Replace all the temporary braces that you removed during this phase of the raising.

The order of raising timbers for the third bent, and especially the fourth, is different because you will have less space to work in. Therefore, have two groups of people working simultaneously to raise the plates, and hold them in place. A third group of people will then bring the bent to the plates.

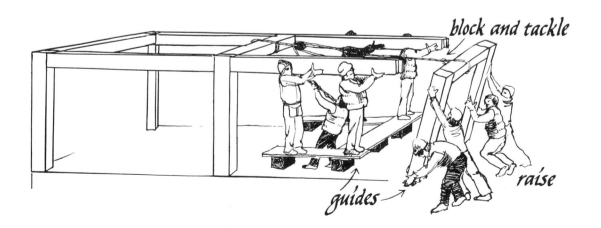

This sequence is followed until the entire second floor system is raised.

Next, lay the joists.

If you are not planning to have plaster ceilings and you want to conceal your electrical wiring, now is the time to rout out a canal in the top surface of your plates, girts and/or summer, and then to lay the wires. Bore down through a timber at any point where you are planning to install a fixture. Make sure to leave enough wire at either end to make the final electrical connections. (Be sure also to check your local electrical codes.)

*route out for wire*

*an example for a hanging light in center of summer*

Next, lay the second floor deck.

If you are raising a cape, or your bents were two stories tall, you are now ready to raise the rafters. If your house is a two-story, with single story posts, repeat the preceding steps for the second story framing.

### Rafters

The raising of rafters is complicated by the fact that you will be working 9 to 18 feet off the ground. We have found that the best method for getting the timbers up is to tie ropes to the near end and to use two sets of people pulling and lifting/pushing.

*2 or 3 people*

*top deck*

*rope*

*1st deck*

*timber*

If your rafters are particularly heavy, or your work force is limited, you could rig a boom off the top deck and use a block and tackle. Be sure to secure the boom tightly with adequate bracing. In determining the height of the boom, you must take into account the space the block and tackle and its ropes holding the timber will need.

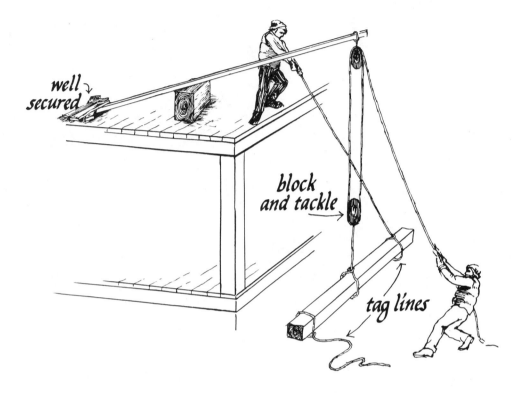

Use ropes as tag lines tied to the ends of the rafter. These are held by people on the ground who are guiding the timber and by people on the deck who are pulling the timber. Raise the timber parallel to the wall, and then turn it 90 degrees to get it onto the deck.

This system requires careful coordination of all the work groups. Leave the purlins on the ground at this point to give yourselves maximum working space. Once all the rafters are on the deck, you are ready to proceed. Tack some blocks to the outside of the frame on the gable end and the side to prevent the rafter from sliding off or spreading too far. Begin at one gable end, and lay the rafters down on the deck with the birdsmouths at their respective locations.

Join the rafters at the peak and peg the joint. Set the collar tie if there is one. Tie a string to the peak. This will serve as a plumb line when the rafter has been raised. Then the first set can be a reference point for the other sets.

One person should stand at each foot to act as a guide. Several people will be needed to do the lifting, and one person should hold the end of a tag line tied to the peak. If the rafters are quite long, you may also need to use the pikes. If distance "a" is less than half the vertical height of the rise, you do not need pikes.

The people at the feet are very important because they prevent the rafters from sliding away or spreading. The birdsmouth joint is also special because it will not be properly situated in position until the rafters are almost completely upright.

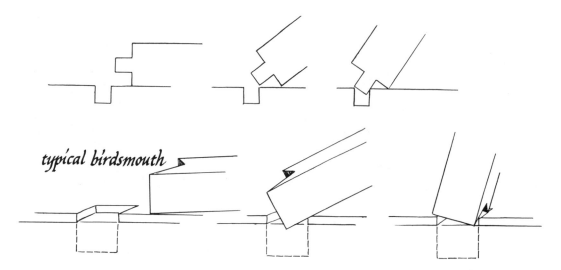

typical birdsmouth

Your overriding fear will be that the rafters will be raised too far and be pushed over. The fear is usually great enough that the problem becomes one of *not* raising the rafters far enough to be plumb. The tag lines offer further security against the rafters going overboard. Temporarily brace this first rafter pair by tacking a board to the underside, or inside, of the rafter, and to the plate.

Then proceed to raise, and brace the remaining sets until you have two sets left. The last set must be raised under the second-to-last set. Therefore, the peak of the pair must be able to pass under any collar tie that might be there. If it will not, then the collar tie for the second-to-last set of rafters must be set after the last gable pair is raised.

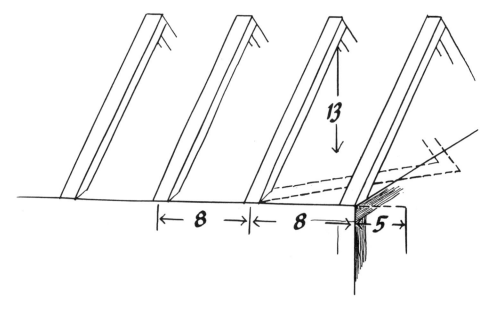

It is probably approaching the end of the day, so while these last pairs of rafters are being raised, ask some people in the crew to begin to set the purlins. Do not nail any of them in at this point.

Once these are set, the ridge pole is handed up and set in place. Now is the time to check the roof rafters as a whole for plumb. Use a come along to align the rafters in their final position and nail or peg the purlins and ridge poles in place. Securely brace the system in the correct position until the permanent braces are set.

The whole process will probably take a full day. Now that you are near the end of this productive day of work, it is time to attach the *pine bough* to the peak of the first set of rafters raised. This tradition is attributed to three sources. One source claims that the old-timers wanted to pay homage to nature for producing the trees from which they built their homes. Another says that the pine bough was a symbol that the colonists' house was "free," and did not belong to the king. A third source says that the tree was homage to god, placed at the highest point of the house in order to be closer to the heavens. To us, the pine bough is representative of all these ideas, but stands primarily as a symbol that the frame has been safely and successfully raised and the time of celebration can begin.

The next day, some of the crew should return to set the permanent braces. See Chapter 8 for a complete discussion of cutting and setting braces.

Once the braces are all in place, the frame is officially complete. You can now proceed with the process of closing in the frame to make it weather-tight.

# 12 FRAME DESIGN AND YOUR TIMBER ORDER

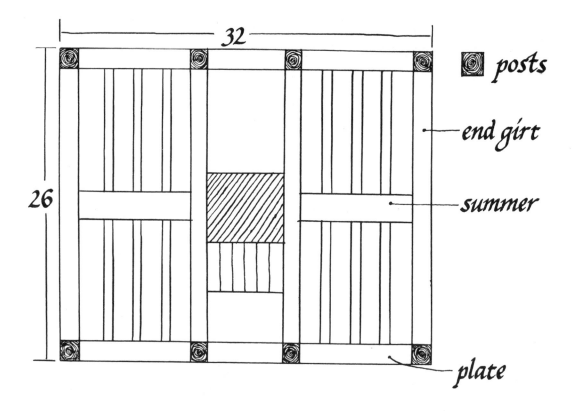

Historically, the frame plan of New England central chimney buildings was quite standardized. The sills in most houses were generally one size, the girts another, and so on. What could vary were the distances between the major girts and plates, and the style of the frame.

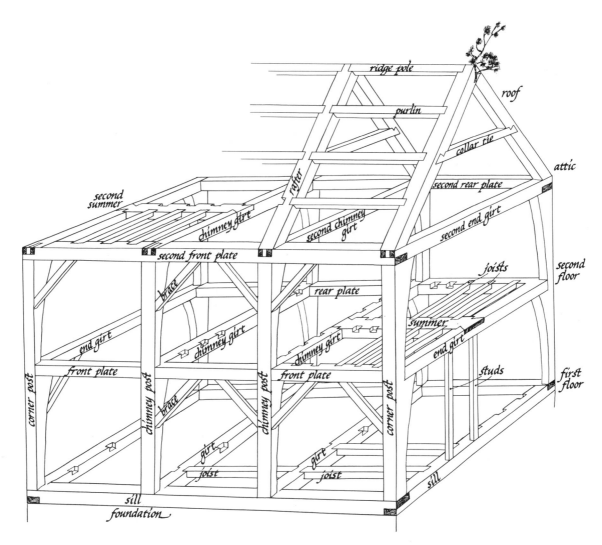

Not much room was left for variety or individual taste. We, however, can design our frames to reflect our own taste while still retaining the characteristics of the traditional frame. For example, we can choose to use a small number of large joists, or a large number of small ones, depending on what effect we would like for the ceiling. It is necessary to understand some of the properties of wood so that you can make design decisions that will ensure a sturdy structure.

Wood standing on end (for instance, a post) is extremely strong. It is easy for a post to bear the forces of compression to which it is subject. For example, pine can support six hundred pounds per square inch. Therefore, a 4'' x 4'' pine post can carry 9,600 pounds. The frame and decks of a 26' x 32' cape weigh approximately 42,560 pounds. Theoretically, the entire house frame could be supported by five 4'' x 4''s! It would jiggle a bit, but it would be supported. Or, how about supporting the frame on one 10'' x 10'' post? It would wobble even more, but it would be able to bear the weight. If you choose to design your frame plan by calculating the loads your house must support, remember that the dimensions of conventional lumber are smaller than the dimensions of timbers ordered from a mill. For example, a 4'' x 4'' will actually measure around 3½'' x 3½'', and therefore, will actually carry 7,350 pounds.

Wood lying on its side has another set of characteristics. A 1" x 6" board laid flat will sag under its own weight. However, if you lay that same board on its edge, it becomes quite strong. Conventional builders often nail two or more boards together to create a strong unit. A timber, however, is a solid mass of wood and therefore is stronger, inch for inch, than a board. Two 2" x 10" boards nailed together are not as strong as one 4" x 10" timber. The strength and sturdiness of a timber frame, then, derives from the fact that timbers are laid on their edges. An interesting rule of thumb for determining the strength of different sized timber is this: for every 2 inches of a timber's height, its strength increases by the ratio of the 2 inches to the original height. For example, a 4" x 8" timber will be one-third stronger than a 4" x 6", the fraction being the result of the ratio of the 2 inches to the original height of 6 inches. However, increasing the width of a timber by 2 inches only increases the strength of the timber by some 10 to 15 percent.

*Architectural Graphic Standards* by Ramsey and Sleeper is your best guide for determining what timbers can span what distances without support. Their charts take into account the species of wood, the live and dead floor loads, and the deflection, or sagging. For example, if code standards for building limit floor deflection to 1/360 of the length of the timber, then a 10 foot timber should not deflect more than 1/3 inch when carrying a 40 pound load. According to their book, many parts of the traditional timber frame are undersized and many parts are oversized. Yet, these frames have stood for three hundred years and more. Study particularly the section in their book on wood lintels and beams.

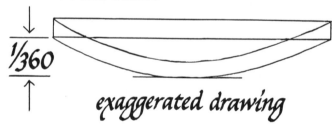

**1/360** *exaggerated drawing*

You must also consider the work the timbers will be doing when you design your frame plan. For example, how many other timbers will be joining any one timber and what are their sizes? Since the summer timber will be joined to the girts, it must be smaller in its vertical dimension than the girt it joins.

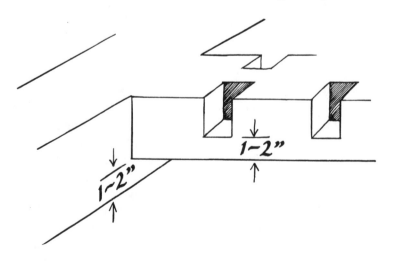

1–2"    1–2"

Similarly, the joists will join the summer. There must be 2 inches of wood beneath the joist pockets to insure that the timber retains its strength. With an understanding of wood properties, the work the timbers must do and the local building codes, you can move on to the process of designing your particular frame plan. The first and most basic decision you make concerns the size of your house. Decide what your overall space requirements are, without committing yourself to window or door placement or to the specific placements of partitions for rooms. Interior design decisions are best left for the time after the frame is raised, when you can experience the house space as it really is. Decide instead how much overall floor space you need, and how many stories you want. Decide on the style of the roof, and its pitch.

The two interior design questions that should be considered as you plan your frame are where the stairs will be located, and where the fireplace(s) will be located. Stairs in old houses were very steep. They often rose at a 40 or 45 degree angle between central girts that were only 7 to 9 feet apart. Colonial builders designed them this way because it was too expensive to heat extra space and because they did not want to sacrifice room space for a larger stair well. Their furniture was smaller (as were they), and their indoor activity was centered around the keeping room downstairs. Stairs as we know them are a fairly recent phenomenon. The old design is considered uncomfortable, unsafe, and impractical. Therefore, when you design your frame, you can allow as much as 10 feet between the central girts for stairs that will have a comfortable incline.

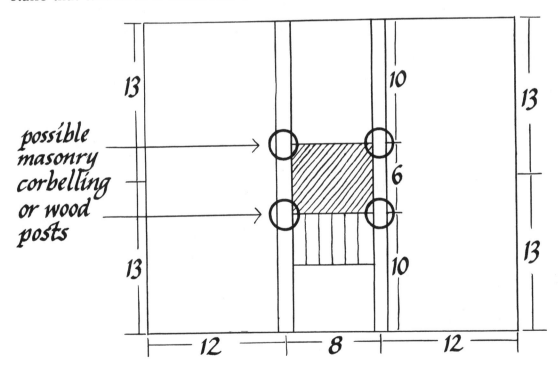

Central fireplaces were a necessity in colonial times. The size and number of fireplaces diminished as charcoal, coal and oil supplemented wood fuel. Today, if you choose to use electric heat, there is really no need for a chimney. However, the high cost of modern fuel is motivating more people to heat with wood in a properly designed fireplace or wood stove. If you are planning to use your fireplace for a heat source, you should locate it in the center of your space. Allow 4 to 8 feet of space for each fireplace. A large, traditional kitchen fireplace with beehive ovens would require a space of 10 feet.

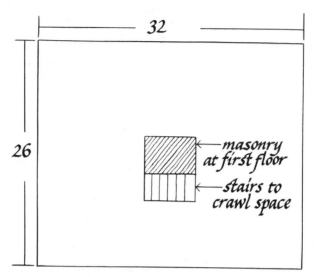

Once you have placed the stairs and masonry on your frame plan, the rest of the timbers are simply "built" around them. For example, the space on either side of the central girts can be as large or as small as you choose. You can now complete your frame plan and make up a timber order. Begin with the first floor frame. Draw the perimeter of your house. (We will use a 26' x 32' cape as our example.) Next, draw the two chimney girts from the front of the frame to the back. We have placed ours 8 feet apart, 12 feet from each end, a plan that will allow for both a central staircase and up to three fireplaces. In our example, we are centering this space.

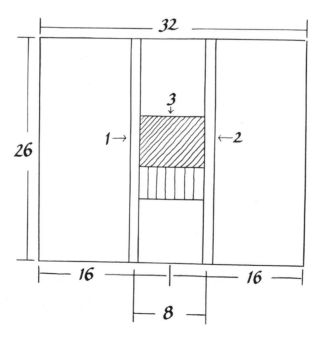

Next, draw in the timbers that will make up the sills.

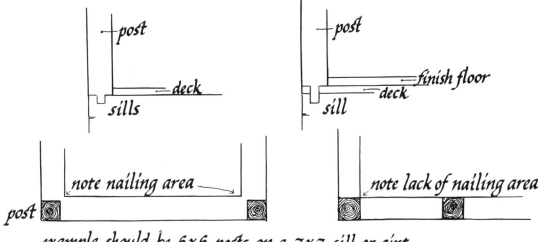

*example should be 6x6 posts on a 7x7 sill or girt*

The last members to complete the first floor frame are the joists. We placed ours on 2 foot centers in all the areas except those which the masonry and staircase will occupy. From this drawing, we can determine our timber order for the first floor frame.

> Sills — 8" x 8" - 4/13, 4/12, 2/10
> Girts — 8" x 10" - 2/26 or 4/14
> > Note: These 26 foot 8" x 10" timbers must be supported by either masonry or posts.
> Joists — 4" x 8" - 24/12, 9/8

This order is read, "sills, eight-by-eights, four thirteen-footers, four twelve-footers, and two ten-footers."

The second floor frame is made up of posts, plates, girts, summers, and joists. In our example, there are eight posts, one placed at each major intersection of major timbers.

The plates and girts are placed as follows.

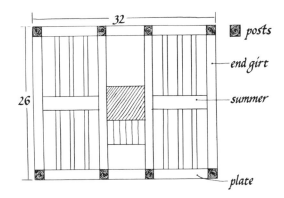

After drawing in the east and west summers, we can finally draw the joists. In our example, these lie in the opposite direction from the first floor joists; they are traditionally placed on 2 foot or 30 inch centers. The timber order for the second floor frame will be as follows.

Girts — 7" x 9" - 4/26

    Note: These 26 foot 7" x 9" timbers must be supported by either masonry or wall framing.

Plates — 7" x 9" - 4/12, 2/8

Posts— 7" x 9" - 8/8

Summers — 8" x 12" - 2/12

Joists — 6" x 6" - 20/13 (2 foot centers)

                16/13 (30 inches centers)

                12/13 (3 foot centers)

If you want your joists on 2 foot centers, you can put down a 1 inch tongue and groove subfloor and then lay the 1 inch tongue and groove finish floor at a later date if you wish. If you choose to place your joists on up to 4 foot centers, you must lay 2 inch tongue and groove deck to ensure adequate load support.

When you place your order, order all like sizes together. For example, simply order 7" x 9" — 10/8, 4/12, 4/26 for the plates, posts and girts.

Repeat this order tally for any other floors if you are building a two story house.

The roof frame order is made up of rafters, purlins, collar ties, and ridge pole. Rafters in our example are placed on 8 foot centers, and the purlins on 4 foot centers. Therefore, there are five pairs of rafters and 32 purlins, and four sections of ridge pole.

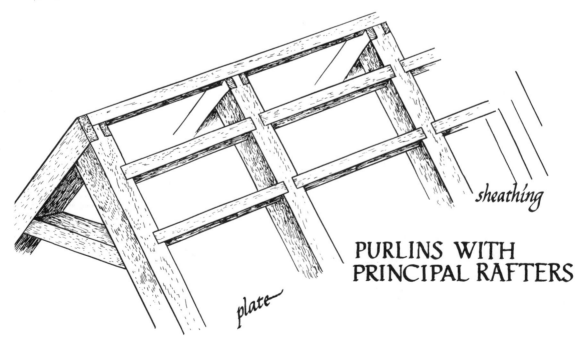

*sheathing*

**PURLINS WITH PRINCIPAL RAFTERS**

*plate*

Refer to Chapter 5 and Chapter 9 to compute the rafter length for your house. In our example, the rafters are 18'5'' and we will order 19 or 20 foot timbers for them.

If you are having collar ties, you must compute their lengths. You can do this by determining how high off the deck they will be. In our example, the rise is 13 feet. If you want the tie to be 7 feet off the deck, there would be 6 feet of space above it. Using our knowledge of algebra and triangles, it is easy to see that 6 feet is one-half the collar tie length, and that we will need a 12 foot timber for the collar tie.

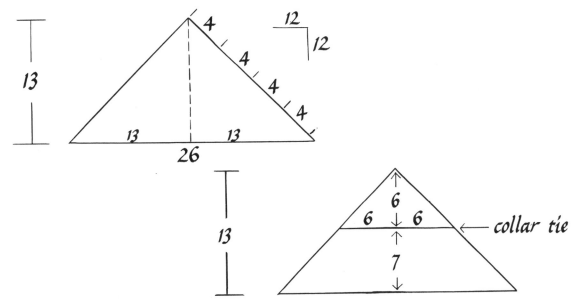

The timber order for the roof system will be as follows.

> *Rafters* — 6'' x 8'' - 10/19 or 10/20
> *Purlins and Ridge* — 4'' x 4'' - 36/8
> *Collar Ties* — 4'' x 8'' - 5/12

Finally, you will need to order braces. Order two braces, each 4 feet long, for every outside post.

> *Braces* 4'' x 4'' - 16/8
> (Combine the brace order with the 8' — 4'' x 4''s you are ordering for purlins and ridge pole.)

Remember that you can vary the sizes of your timbers and the distances between them, but be sure you have considered deflection, live and dead loads, local code requirements, and the joinery each timber will contain. Again, we can help you with your timber plan and order in a number of ways if you are unsure about doing it by yourself. We can draw your plan if we know the statistics of your house, and you can figure out your order. Or, we can do both drawing and the order. Or, you can send us your plan and order and we can check it over. You can also send us your plan and ask how you can vary the size of certain timbers to meet your design needs. Write to us for details regarding such consultation.

# 13 BUILDING A 12' x 16' SHED

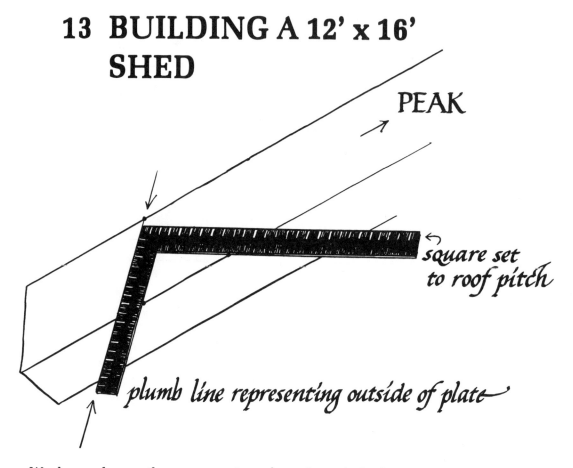

PEAK

square set
to roof pitch

plumb line representing outside of plate

We have chosen the construction of a 12' x 16' shed as a practice project for several reasons. First, building a small structure is an ideal way to become accustomed to working with timbers. Second, the shed is big enough to be useful during the construction of your main house as a tool shed, or even living space. And third, it will be a useful size for an outbuilding shop, studio, one-car garage, or small barn. We are going to design the building from the ground up. We have overdesigned the structure of this shed in order to include many of the joints that you will need to construct a larger structure. Thus, there is a summer timber in our shed, though there would not usually be one for a building this size. We conclude this chapter with the personal account of a friend of ours who is now on the staff of Housesmiths. He built this shed without having much prior experience in timber framing, by using the frame drawings and timber schedules we have included in this chapter.

Beginning with the foundation, we suggest that you set the shed on concrete or stone piers. Using piers will minimize your initial costs and will not scar the earth. It will also allow you the flexibility to move the shed to a better location in the future.

We understand that as the complex of buildings and landscaping grows, the original site of the shed may not be satisfactory. Therefore, the shed will be able to be jacked up slightly, set on skids, and dragged to another location.

We also suggest that you use 2 inch planks for the first floor in order to give the shed enough rigidity to serve as a shop. These planks can support heavy equipment. The second deck can consist of 1 inch boards to support lighter storage or a sleeping loft. The doors and windows can be put any place except where there is a timber or brace. The final covering of clapboards, shingles or boards can be delayed until later to offset the initial expenses. The roof need only be covered with some waterproof material to keep the interior dry during the initial phase of use.

Now, for the specifications. We have chosen the 12' x 16' base measurement with an 8 foot wall, a 12/12 roof pitch (square), and a summer timber. Here are the descriptions of the foundation plan, the timber frame drawings including elevations, and the timber schedules. (Drawings begin on page 150.)

### Foundation Plan

Consider the future use of the building, access during construction, levelness, dryness, and stability of the soil when selecting your site. Remove enough topsoil and make your foundation level with the highest point on your site. To check the piers for squareness, the diagonal measurements must be equal.

### Timber Frame Drawings

These drawings show the overall frame plan from the front of the frame, the end of the frame, and from above the frame. There are also drawings which show some of the detail of some of the joinery in the frame.

### Timber Schedules

The timber drawings, or schedules, show the name, size, length, and quantity needed of that particular timber, the dimensions of each of its joints, and the location of the timber in the frame.

*Roman numerals* (I, II, etc.) and *capital letters* (A, B-B, etc.) indicate where the timber goes in the frame. The order of these numerals and letters is significant. For example, in the code "A-B," the "A" is the left end of the timber when it is in place, as pictured, in the frame, and "B" is the right end. These numerals and letters correspond to identical ones on the frame drawings. For example, a corner post shown on a timber schedule and coded "D" will match with a plate labeled "C-D" and a girt labeled "D-B" on the frame drawing. All the ends of these timbers labeled "D" will meet at the joint over the post labeled "D."

> *6 x 6 - 18* means the timbers are 6 inches by 6 inches and are 18 feet long.
>
> *2 PC.* means you need two pieces of the item shown in the drawing for your frame.

*Sill* is the name of the timber shown.

*18'0" OAL* means that the particular dimension given is for the overall length of the timber.

℄ means center line for the joint.

*c.s.* means to make a rough but square cut with a chain saw.

The order of the dimensions given for a joint is important. For example, a mortise that is 4 x 4 x 2 is 4 inches *wide*, 4 inches *high*, and 2 inches *deep*.

Here is the material list of the timbers and lumber needed to frame the shed.

### First Floor

sills — 6 x 10 - 2/16, 2/12
joists — 6 x 8 - 7/12

### Second Floor

posts — 6 x 6 - 4/10
girts — 6 x 10 - 2/12
plates — 6 x 10 - 2/16
summer — 8 x 12 - 1/16
joists — 6 x 6 - 6/6 (or 3/12)

### Roof

rafters — 6 x 6 - 6/10
purlins — 4 x 4 - 10/8

### Braces, Window and Door Framing, Nailers

4 x 4 - 20/8

### Trenails

40 — 1 inch by 8 inch diameter
80 — ½ inch by 6 inch diameter

### Decking

2 inch tongue and groove pine
192 square feet or 384 board feet, plus 40 board feet for waste and milling
1 inch tongue and groove pine
192 square feet, or 192 board feet plus 20 board feet for waste and milling

After you have studied all the drawings, proceed to cut your timbers. You can develop your own system for doing this, as we suggested in the laying out and cutting chapters. Be sure to take into account any boxing that will be needed. Check the measurements of each timber as you go so that you do not repeat a mistake. Refer often to the drawings, and keep the entire frame in mind as you cut each timber.

Next comes the raising. We suggest that you lay the first floor framing and the deck some time before your friends assemble to help you raise. This will give you all something to walk on and work off of for a more efficient and safer raising. Be sure that you check the overall dimensions for accuracy at each level. The base measure must remain 12' x 16' on the outside, and all measurements must be square, plumb and level. You can use shims between the foundation and the frame to help level the sills. It is imperative that the first floor deck be level and square. The rest of the building will be off if you don't make sure these initial measurements are accurate.

Although we do not examine the closing in of a timber frame in this book, we would like to give you a few directions for your shed. Sheathing a timber frame differs from sheathing a conventional frame because the sheathing boards are nailed vertically, not horizontally. You will need 576 board feet, plus waste, of 1 inch boards to sheathe the shed. Subtract the area that your windows and doors will occupy before ordering. You will need 302 board feet of 1 inch boards to sheathe the roof. Apply the roof boards from ridge to plate, that is, vertically, as you did the wall sheathing.

We think the specifics of cutting and raising this shed can best be presented by a novice who actually did it using only a little previously acquired conventional carpentry skill and the drawings. This is Arthur Hendrick's journal of the event.

> I had been working with Housesmiths for about a week and had seen only a couple of timber frame buildings when Stewart Elliott asked me if I'd like to cut and raise a frame myself. Never having taken part in the building of this type of house, I was doubtful of my abilities. I agreed to give it a try. My background in construction had been eight months with a conventional, stud-frame company, so I was familiar with the tools of the trade, but the particulars of the post and beam method were completely different from anything I had done.
>
> The cloud of doubt began to clear when Stewart brought out drawings of the building. The shed was to house several chickens and a three-year-old Welsh pony named Pony.
>
> The drawings included each timber with all the necessary dimensions, joints and locations. It looked simple, and I was assured that it was.
>
> Not knowing exactly how to go about cutting a frame, I went down to the field to begin. Like a soldier going to battle, I was armed. I had a power saw, a large power drill, a four point hand saw, a 2 inch wide socket chisel, a mallet, a 2 foot square, tape measure and carpenter's pencil.
>
> I began with the joists because they looked easy. Their ends only had to be squared to proper length. A little pile of finished joists bolstered my confidence so that I jumped into the girts and posts next, completing the mortise and tenon joints. I did the summer dovetail joint last.
>
> The cutting of the posts, girts, rafters and the summer went smoothly and rapidly. The only real problem arose when I cut the girts before I cut the summer. The dovetail pocket in the girt that receives the summer is cut exactly to match the dimensions of the 8" x 12" piece of wood being put into it.

Wood, however, is imperfect. There can be variations of up to ¼ inch. After cutting one end girt and its pocket for the summer, I found that the summer measured 11¾ inches, not 12 inches. Hence, I had a gap in the finished frame on one side of the summer joint. Fortunately this happened only on one end; because I had not yet cut the other girt, I was able to make it fit more precisely. I learned my lesson: cut the summer timber tenons *before* you cut their corresponding pockets in the girts. You may need to do some customizing. This order of cutting also helps to mark the matching joints. This removes the possibility of having to take the summer down to rotate it. This would not be an easy chore with a 16 foot 8" x 12"!

My horse shed was cut and stacked, and awaiting its raising. I placed the sills on six 4 foot posts that I had buried about a yard deep and leveled with a transit. When the sills were securely pegged, we laid the floor joists and checked for square by cross-measuring the floor. Then the decks were applied, making a floor that could support just about anything. The shed sat like this for a few days while I rounded up people to help raise it.

The raising of my horse shed began a little behind schedule on this November day. In fact, it was just before dusk! The nearing darkness wasn't much of a problem, though, as lots of people had come to help. It's funny how many people are attracted to a bunch of folks scurrying around trying to assemble a large, three-dimensional puzzle in the dark, seemingly supervised by an impatient Welsh pony. The throng and the fun quickly turned the ridge pole party into a summer timber party. This isn't as bad as a basement sill party, but it's not exactly what our timber-frame forefathers had in mind. Or, was it?

The shed climbed swiftly higher. The four corner posts and the plates and girts were soundly braced and pegged together, and waiting for the summer. The summer was a particularly heavy timber, and it soon became clear that all the helpers on hand would be needed to hoist it to its final resting place, 7 feet above the deck. So hoist we did. Ten backs and 20 arms and the summer was home and she was tight.

From there it seemed only minutes until the joists were inserted, the rafters pegged together and the purlins firmly nailed. The ridge pole and the traditional pine bough were up and the frame was done!

Complete darkness had fallen by then, so I couldn't see my raised frame, but I knew from sitting on the ridge pole that the horse shed was strong and, even in the dark, beautiful. There had been a few errors in my cutting, but nothing that couldn't be taken care of with a little extra cutting or a few blows with the sledge hammer. I had a tremendous feeling of elation sitting on the ridge pole. The frame was up — strong, handsome, traditional, and surprisingly simple.

Now you have studied this book and are ready to begin building either the practice shed or your house frame. We hope that what we have written in this book tells you all you'll need to know to build a timber frame. If you feel confident about your math skills but not your carpentry, you can send us the specifications and drawings for your frame and we can cut your timbers for you. We can then either ship them to you or you can pick them up. Then, you and your friends can raise the frame. If you do not feel confident about raising the frame, one or more of us can come to your site to supervise your crew, or ours. We are always eager to answer questions and letters from the folks who have read this book and are building themselves a timber frame. Please write to us if you would like price quotations on drawings, timber cutting, or raisings. Thank you for your interest in timber framing and best of luck!

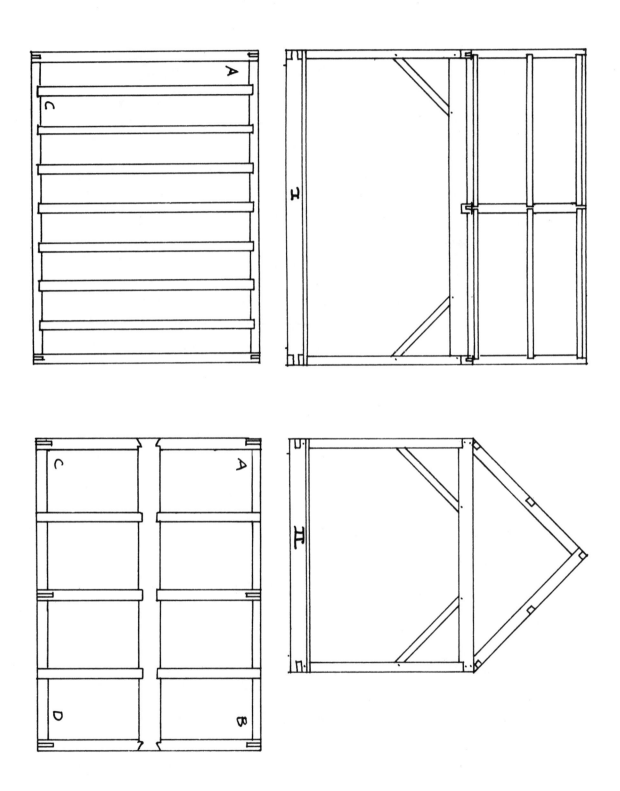

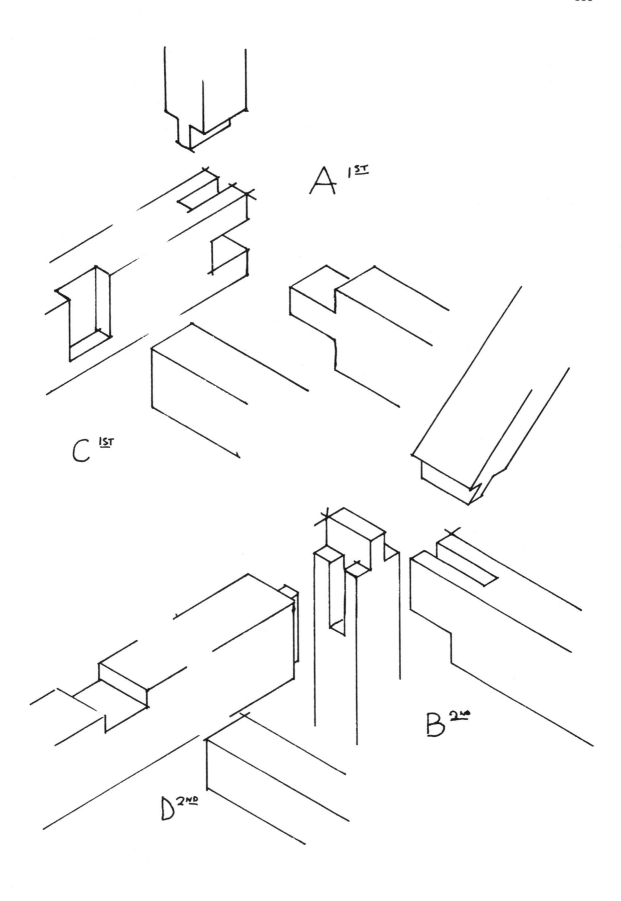

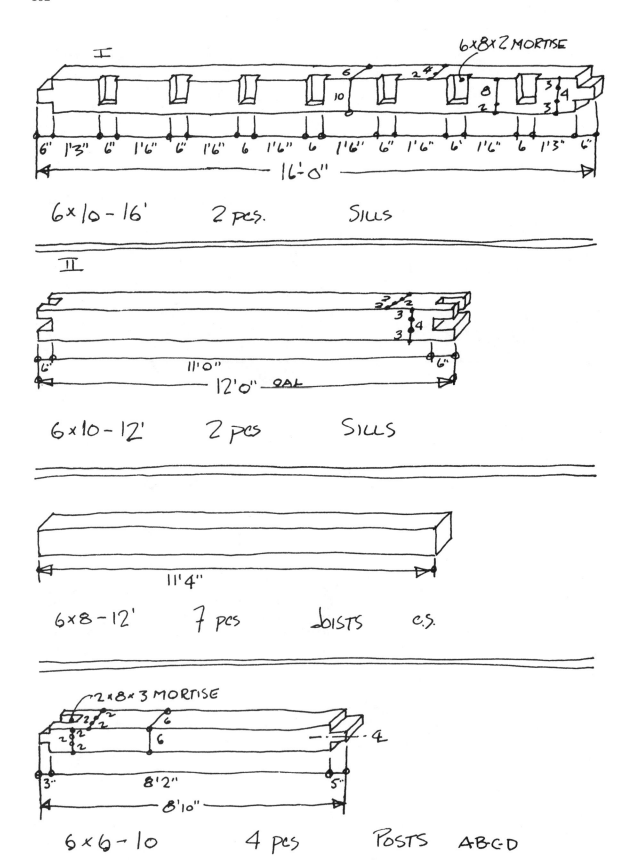

I

6×8×2 MORTISE

6      24

10

8
2

3
3      4

6"  1'3"  6"  1'6"  6"  1'6"  6"  1'6"  6"  1'6"  6"  1'6"  6'  1'6"  6"  1'3"  6"

16'-0"

6×10 - 16'        2 pcs.        SILLS

II

3    2
3

3    4
3

6"           11'0"                6"
        12'0"   OAL

6×10 - 12'      2 pcs       SILLS

11'4"

6×8 - 12'       7 pcs       JOISTS      C.S.

2×8×3 MORTISE

2
2  2
2  2      6
2

6      --4

3"        8'2"        5"
        8'10"

6×6 - 10        4 pcs       POSTS    A-B-C-D

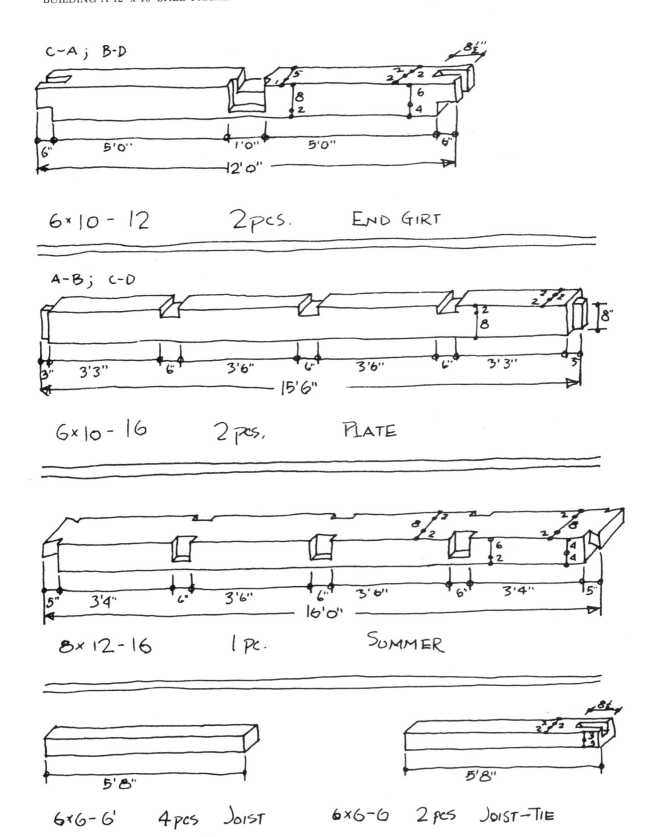

C-A ; B-D

6×10 - 12      2 pcs.      END GIRT

A-B ; C-D

6×10 - 16      2 pcs,      PLATE

8×12-16      1 pc.      SUMMER

6×6-6'   4 pcs   JOIST          6×6-6   2 pcs   JOIST—TIE

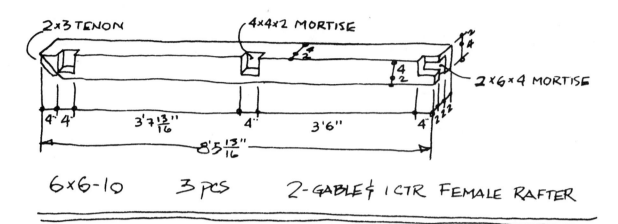

2×3 TENON   4×4×2 MORTISE   2×6×4 MORTISE

4'  4'   3' 7 13/16"   4"   3'6"   4"

8' 5 13/16"

6×6-10     3 PCS     2-GABLE & 1 CTR FEMALE RAFTER

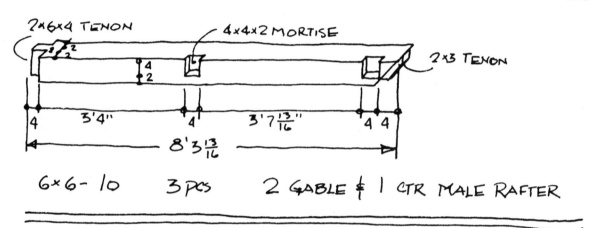

2×6×4 TENON   4×4×2 MORTISE   2×3 TENON

4"   3'4"   4"   3' 7 13/16"   4"  4"

8' 3 13/16"

6×6-10     3 PCS     2 GABLE & 1 CTR MALE RAFTER

4×4-8     10 PCS     PURLINS & RIDGE POLE
C.S. to 7'7" O.A.L.

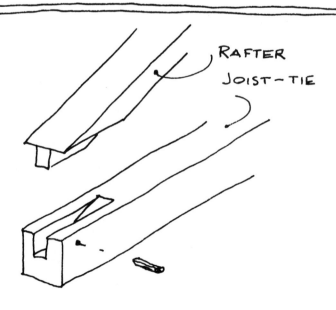

RAFTER

JOIST-TIE

# BIBLIOGRAPHY

This bibliography is a small sampling of useful books since there are literally hundreds of books available that would be helpful. We feel that as an owner-builder or interested party, you should have as much participation as possible in the design and execution of your home. Reading and research are an important foundation to such participation. Therefore, in addition to the bibliography, we would like to mention some general sources of good publications which will help you make your home a very personal statement.

First, check into the universities and colleges in your area. They may offer their resources to their community at reasonable rates. Also, check with the Extension Service for pamphlets related to building. There are also several groups starting their own schools to teach people how to build their own homes. Most of these are contemporary in their design philosophy and are particularly concerned with energy conservation. The federal and state government supply various sources of information, most of which are free or very inexpensive. In particular, the Library of Congress sponsors one program that is of special interest to us. The Historical American Building Survey offers measured drawings and photos of extinct and existing historical houses. In order to order these, you need the catalogues which list the houses for which plans are available. These can be obtained by writing to the Library of Congress Photoduplication Service, 10 1st St. SE, Washington, D.C., 20540. Request information on how to order the "Catalogues of the Measured Drawings and Photographs of the Survey in the Library of Congress," March 1, 1941, and January 1959, #PB 177 632 and 633. These are extensive and expensive catalogues containing descriptions of thousands of homes. Smaller catalogues listing historical homes by the state are also available. State, local and private preservation groups are also a source of information.

ANDERSON, L. O. *How to Build a Wood-Frame House*. New York, New York: Dover Publications, Inc., 1973.
    A good conventional "how to" for all standard residential construction. Concerned with all phases of construction.
BLACKBURN, GRAHAM. *Illustrated Housebuilding*. Woodstock, New York: The Overlook Press, 1974.
BOERICKE, ART, and SHAPIRO, BARRY. *Handmade Houses, a Guide to the Woodbutcher's Art*. San Francisco, California: Scrimshaw Press, 1973.
    An entertaining, pictorial, artsy book.
THE COLONIAL WILLIAMSBURG FOUNDATION. *A Portfolio of Eighty-Eight Original Williamsburg Buildings*. New York: Holt, Rinehart, and Winston, 1971.

ECCLI, EUGENE. *Low-Cost, Energy-Efficient Shelter for the Owner and Builder.* Emmaus, Pennsylvania: Rodale Press, Inc., 1975.
   This book contains the writings of many talented people. Though principally concerned with energy and cost, much of the information is applicable. It's loaded with ideas.

FIELDS, CURTIS P. *The Forgotten Art of Building a Stone Wall.* Dublin, New Hampshire: Yankee, Inc., 1971.

FITCH, JAMES M. *American Building.* New York: Schocken Books, 1966.

HOWELLS, JOHN MEAD. *The Architectural Heritage of the Piscataqua.* New York: Architectural Book Publishing Co., Inc., 1965.

KAHN, LLOYD. *Shelter.* Bolinas, California: Shelter Publications, 1973.

KAINS, M. G. *Five Acres and Independence.* New York, New York: Dover Publications, Inc., 1973.
   Explores more land uses and self-sufficiency, but not much usable information for it is hard to have a house and no land.

KAUFMANN, HENRY. *The American Farm House.* New York: Hawthorn Books, Inc., 1975.

KELLY, J. FREDERICK. *Early Domestic Architecture of Connecticut.* New York, New York: Dover Publications, Inc., 1952.
   This is the first book I've read that actually historically studied the component parts of the early homes — including the frame.

KERN, KEN. *The Owner-Built Home.* Auberry, California: Homestead Press, 1972.
   Siting, costs, and alternate methods are the main sources of information.

KERN, KEN. *The Owner-Built Homestead.* Auberry, California: Homestead Press, 1972.

KIDDER, SMITH, G. E. *A Pictorial History of Architecture in America.* New York: American Heritage Publishing Co., Inc., 1976.

OLIVER, PAUL. *Shelter and Society.* New York, New York: Frederick A. Praegar, Publishers, 1969.

ORTON, VREST. *The Forgotten Art of Building a Good Fireplace.* Dublin, New Hampshire: Yankee, Inc., 1969.

PRATT, RICHARD. *A Treasury of Early American Homes.* New York, New York: Whittlesey House, 1949.

RAMSEY, CHARLES G., A. I. A., and SLEEPER, HAROLD R., F. A. I. A. *Architectural Graphic Standards.* New York: John Wiley and Sons, Inc., 1956.
   This book is reprinted every several years and updated according to codes, needs, and technology. It's the architects' bible with hundreds of pages of details, charts, and tables. It's expensive, so check your library.

ROBERTS, REX. *Your Engineered House.* New York: M. Evans and Co., Inc., 1964.

ROBINSON, ALBERT G. *Old New England Houses.* New York: Weathervane Books, 1920.

SCOTT, JOHN S. *A Dictionary of Building.* Great Britain: Hazell, Watson, and Viney Ltd., 1974.

SIEGELE, H. H. *Roof Framing.* New York, New York: Drake Publishers, Inc., 1972.
   An excellent and concise source of information on the use of the framing square and understanding roofs.

SLOANE, ERIC. *Our Vanishing Landscape.* New York: Funk and Wagnalls, 1955.

SLOANE, ERIC. *Reverence for Wood.* New York: Funk and Wagnalls, 1965.

SLOANE, ERIC. *The Second Barrel* and *The Cracker Barrel.* New York: Funk and Wagnalls, 1967.

SYLVESTER, W. A. *The Modern House-Carpenter's Companion.* New York: Palliser, Palliser and Co., 1883.
Offers an insight to the history of building with much useful information.

TUNIS, EDWARD. *Colonial Living.* Cleveland, Ohio: The World Publishing Co., 1957.

U. S. DEPARTMENT OF AGRICULTURE. *Trees for Shade and Beauty.* Bulletin 117. Washington, D.C.: U. S. Government Printing Office.

U. S. DEPARTMENT OF AGRICULTURE. *Wood Handbook.* Washington, D.C.: U.S. Government Printing Office, Division of Documents, 1955.

U. S. NAVY, BUREAU OF NAVAL PERSONNEL. *Basic Construction Techniques for Houses and Small Buildings Simply Explained.* New York: Dover Publications, Inc., 1972.

WAGNER, WILLIS H. *Modern Carpentry.* South Holland, Illinois: The Goodheart-Wilcox Co., Inc., 1969.
A good source of conventional methods and materials.

WILLIAMS, CHRISTOPHER. *Craftsmen of Necessity.* New York: First Vintage Books, Random House, 1974.

WILSON, J. DOUGLAS, and ROGERS, CLELL M. *Simplified Carpentry Estimating.* New York, New York: Simmons-Boardman Books, 1960.

# GLOSSARY

**adze** — a tool like an axe used for roughly surfacing a timber.

**auger** — a drilling tool shaped like a corkscrew and used for boring holes in wood.

**backfilling** — replacing the earth around a foundation which was removed during excavation.

**balloon frame** — modern American house construction in which studs run to the roof plate past the floor joists which are nailed to them.

**barn pole** — a long pole with a pointed steel head used in raising bents; also called a pike.

**bead** — a semi-circular molding.

**beetle** — a heavy maul or mallet; should be used in cases in which material would be damaged by a sledge hammer.

**bent** — a section of the frame which is composed of a line of vertical posts and the horizontal timbers that connect them.

**bevel square** — a square with a hinged blade passing through the handle; the angle between the blade and the handle is adjustable.

**birdsmouth** — a V-shaped joint used at the plate end of a rafter.

**blade** — the longer blade of a framing square measuring 24 inches long and 2 inches wide, also called the body.

**block and tackle** — a set of bulky, solid pieces of wood and ropes used for hoisting.

**board foot** — an abstract measurement for lumber 1 inch thick, 12 inches wide, and 12 inches long.

**body** — the longer blade of a framing square measuring 24 inches in length and 2 inches in width; also called the blade.

**box** — to shave or plane down any portions of a joint which may be oversized.

**braces** — smaller timbers placed diagonally between posts and girts or plates to make a structure more rigid.

**brick nogging** — bricks and clay mortar used to fill in the open areas of the timber frame on the exterior walls; it is covered by clapboards outside, and by plaster inside.

**broad axe** — a wide-edged axe with a cutting bevel on one side only; used for rough dressing a timber.

**broad hatchet** — a wide-edged hatchet with a cutting bevel on one side only; used for rough dressing of a timber or joint.

**buck saw** — a saw set in a deep H-shaped frame for sawing wood on a sawbuck or sawhorse.

**buttress** — a projecting surface designed to support a wall or building; receives the lateral pressure exerted at a particular point in a single direction.

**cape** — a house design of usually 1 to 1½ stories with a straight-run gable roof.

**carpenter's pencil** — a large, flat pencil with soft lead used for marking measurements.

**center line** — the midline on the face of a timber, or joint.

**central tenon** — a tenon that protrudes from the center of the end of a timber.

**champher** — an edge cut off symmetrically at a 45 degree angle.

**circular saw** — an electrical saw with a circular steel disc which has teeth cut round the rim.

**clapboards** — narrow boards thicker at one edge; used as siding.

**collar tie** — the timber parallel to the girts which connects rafter pairs at a given height.

**combination square** — an adjustable tool which can be used as an inside or outside try square, mitre square, plumb rule, and marking gauge.

**come along** — a notched bar with a click works to prevent reversal of motion operating a cable or rope; used for gaining leverage and for pulling timbers together during raising.

**compression** — a force that presses or squeezes.

**concave** — hollow and curved, or rounded.

**conventional frame** — plywood and stud construction.

**convex** — curved or rounded as the exterior of circular form viewed from without.

**corner chisel** — used for cutting out mortises and having an L-shaped blade.

**cribs** — a cradle made of logs for holding other logs during cutting.

**cross brace** — to lay one temporary brace across another, so that the two are tacked together at the point where they cross.

**crown** — a slight convex curve on the face of a timber.

**d** — an abbreviation used with nail sizes; an abbreviation for "penny."

**dead load** — the combined weight of all the materials and all the permanent attachments of a structure.

**deck** — floor.

**deflection** — a bending downward, or sagging.

**dormer** — a vertical window or opening coming through a sloping roof; usually provided with its own pitched roof.

**double-bit axe** — axe with sharp edge running on two sides of the head.

**double-tenoned scarf joint** — a scarf joint without bevel cuts, but with two tenons on each member which run perpendicular to each other; contains a mortise to receive folding wedges (see diagram).

**dovetail** — a joint used to secure the summer timber; has a dovetail-shaped tenon and a corresponding mortise.

**draw knife** — a tool having a blade with a handle at each end; by drawing it toward you, you can shave surfaces.

**dressed-one-side** — a board that has been planed on one side.

**dressed shoulder** — a planed and shaped portion of the joint.

**excavation** — digging of a cavity to make space for a foundation.

**face** — a surface of a timber.

**first floor frame** — sills, girts and joists resting on the foundation.

**flush cut** — an even cut unbroken in one plane.

**forces** — strengths or energies.

**foundation** — wood or masonry support of the building resting on the earth.

**framing chisel** — large chisel with long, heavy blades; strong enough to be hit with a heavy mallet.

**framing square** — an L-shaped metal or metal-and-wood tool for setting out right angles; has a body (or blade) 24 inches long and 2 inches wide, and a tongue 16 inches long and 1½ inches wide.

**full-width tenon** — a tenon that is the same width as the timber from which it projects.

**gable roof** — a sloping roof with one or two triangular-shaped end walls between the rafters.

**gambrel** — a roof design with a lower steeper slope and an upper flatter one; designed so that each gable is pentagonal.

**garrison** — a house design having a second story perimeter larger than the first story perimeter.

**girt** — major horizontal timber which runs from the front to the back of a structure.

**gunstock post** — a special post which provides additional support at the point where other major timbers meet; they widen in size in one traverse direction from floor to ceiling.

**half-dovetail** — this joint is one-half of a dovetail; used for joining collar ties to rafters and braces to posts and for other similar situations.

**half-lap** — a joint having an L-shaped mortise and a corresponding L-shaped tenon.

**half-lap scarf joint** — another term for scarf joint which uses the half-lap as its method of joining, for example, two girts joined end to end (see diagram).

**halved scarf** — a scarf joint splayed down the width of the timber thus creating two beveled surfaces which interlock with the receiving timber (see diagram).

**hand-hewn** — a timber squared off and shaped by hand.

**haunch** — the part of the whole timber beyond the shoulder which is let into another timber.

**haunched half-lap** — a joint with a tenon; full-width part of the whole timber beyond the shoulder is let into another timber, i.e., a dovetail.

**housing** — a mortise.

**inside dimension** — the length of a timber minus the joints on the ends.

**joinery** — the craft of connecting and securing the separate members of the timber frame to one another by means of specific cuts on the ends and/or sides of the timbers.

**joint** — the part, or the arrangement of the part, where two or more timbers are joined together.

**joist** — smaller horizontal timbers which run parallel to each other between major timbers to fill out the structure; provide support for decks.

**kerfs** — saw cuts.

**king post** — posts in a roof which spans more than 36 feet and which are located between the ridge pole and the collar ties.

**knee brace** — a short diagonal timber placed between the horizontal and vertical members of the frame to make them rigid.

**knot** — a place in a tree from which a branch has grown out.

**laying out** — measuring and marking joints and dimensions.

**let in** — to make a shallow sinking in one timber so that it can receive or enclose the end of another.

**letting through** — a method for assembling joints whereby one timber passes completely through another.

**level** — a condition whereby no part of an area or timber is higher than another; on an equal plane.

**level** — a device for determining a horizontal line, having a glass tube nearly filled with alcohol or ether in which is enclosed a moveable bubble; when centered, it determines whether the tangent to the tube at the point or line of sight is truly horizontal.

**linear foot** — a foot measured in a line.

**lintel** — a small beam over a door or window or other openings (such as a fireplace).

**live load** — the load, beyond the load of its own weight, to which a structure is subjected.

**loads** — that which burdens or weighs down something else.

**lofting** — a method for determining measurements by drawing the members full-scale.

**mallet** — a tool like a hammer with a wooden, rawhide or rubber head.

**mason** — one who builds with stone, brick or the like.

**masonry** — anything constructed of stone, brick, tile, or concrete; used by masons.

**matched boards** — tongue and groove or shiplapped boards.

**modified mortise** — an open mortise used for joining rafters at the peak.

**molding plane** — a plane used to cut continuous projections or grooves as decoration.

**mortise and tenon** — any joint consisting of a projection on the end of one timber and a corresponding slot on the other.

**mortising chisel** — a chisel strong enough to be struck with a mallet; used for cutting mortises.

**oilcloth** — cloth soaked in oil and tacked to window openings to let in light but keep out the elements; used in lieu of glass.

**on center** — a method for indicating the spacing of framing members by stating the measurement from the center of one member to the center of the succeeding one.

**outside dimension** — overall length of an uncut timber.

**overhang** — a projection of a roof beyond the wall which carries it.

**overlaying** — a method for assembling timbers whereby one timber is laid on top of another.

**partition** — a wall which separates adjacent rooms.

**peg** — an oak dowel ranging approximately from 5/8 inches to 1½ inches in diameter.

**perimeter** — the whole outer boundary of a structure.

**pike** — a long pole with a pointed steel head used in raising bents; also called a barn pole.

**pin** — a wood peg no larger than 5/8 inches in diameter.

**pine bough** — small portion of a pine tree which, once the whole frame has been raised, should be attached to the peak of the first set of rafters raised.

**pit saw** — a two-man saw used by colonial builders; one man stands in a pit and one stands on level ground to saw.

**plate** — the major second or third story horizontal timber which runs from one end of the frame to the other and supports the rafters.

**plumb** — conforming to a true vertical line.

**plumb bob** — a weight hanging on a string to show the direction of the vertical.

**plumb line** — a string on which a weight is hung in order to stretch the string into a vertical direction.

**pocket** — a mortise.

**points** — moveable buttons for a framing square to set dimensions.

**posts** — upright timbers erected perpendicular to the sills at a corner and at intermediate positions and within the frame, for example, around masonry.

**principal rafters** — these are 5" x 7" to 7" x 9" timbers placed 8 to 12 feet on center and used with either purlins or secondary rafters or alone in some systems of roof rafters; if used alone, they are placed on 3 to 4 foot centers.

**purlin** — a horizontal member of the roof frame which runs between rafters.

**Pythagorus's formula** — a formula for determining the lengths of sides of right triangles; useful in computing rafter and brace measurements: $a^2 + b^2 = c^2$.

**queen posts** — the two posts nearest the midspan of a truss which spans 35 to 70 feet.

**rabbet plane** — a plane with a cutting iron and mouth reaching to the edge of the smooth undersurface; used for cutting long step-shaped rectangular recesses in the edge of a timber.

**rafter** — sloping main timber of the roof frame.

**relieve** — chop or chisel out a portion of wood in a joint.

**ridge** — the horizontal apex of the roof.

**ridge pole** — horizontal timber which connects rafter pairs at the peak.

**rigid** — stiff and immobile in respect to itself.

**rip saw** — a saw for cutting with the wood grain.

**rise** — the vertical height from the supports to the ridge of a roof.

**roof pitch** — a ratio of the height of the ridge to the span of the building.

**run** — one-half the width of a building.

**saltbox** — a house design named for its roof which is composed of two shed roofs having unequal pitches.

**sawyer** — one whose occupation it is to saw.

**scarf joint** — a joint made by champhering, halving, notching, or otherwise cutting away, two pieces so that they correspond to each other, overlapping them, and then securing them with bolts, pegs, or the like.

**score** — to scratch or etch a mark.

**scribing** — shaping one member to the surface which it touches, for example, to fit a board snugly to a surface which is not straight.

**secondary rafters** — these are 4" x 5" or 4" x 6" timbers placed 20 to 30 inches on center; used with principal rafters in one system of roof rafters.

**sheathing** — the first covering of boards or waterproof material on the outside walls and roof.

**shim** — a thin slip of wood, metal or stone, often tapered; used to fill in, as in leveling a timber.

**shoulder** — the area of the void created when the waste around a tenon has been cut away.

**side** — the larger dimension of a given timber.

**sill** — major horizontal timbers which lie on the foundation and form the lowest part of the frame.

**single-bit axe** — axe with sharp edge on one side of the head.

**sledge** — a large, heavy hammer.

**slope** — the degree of deviation from the horizontal or perpendicular; an incline.

**socket chisel** — a massive chisel, with a socket at the base into which the wood handle fits; used for mortising; it is strong enough to be struck with a mallet.

**smooth-one-side** — a board that has been planed on one side.

**span** — the width of a building.

**square** — an L-shaped metal or metal and wood tool used to set out right angles.

**square** — a true parallelogram, having four equal sides and four right triangles.

**square foot** — the measurement of an area of 144 square inches.

**square off** — to cut at a right angle.

**square pitch** — a roof pitch in which rafters meet at right angles at the peak.

**stable** — steady and immobile in respect to the earth.

**staging** — scaffolding.

**stepping off** — a system for determining rafter lengths and cuts.

**stop** — decorative end of a champher.

**straight-run roof** — a roof on which the principal parts are arranged in a straight line.

**stress** — pressure or strain.

**subfloor** — a 1 inch floor which carries the load; eventually covered by a finish floor.

**summer** — a major horizontal timber which spans the girts, ranging in width from 12 to 17½ inches.

**tabled scarf joint** — similar to a double-tenoned scarf, the only difference being that one of the tenons is beveled (see diagram).

**tag line** — a rope tied to the ends of a timber being lifted to keep it from swinging from side to side.

**tail** — the end portion of a birdsmouth joint which extends beyond the plate when there is a roof overhang.

**tapered post** — a post that is 2 to 4 inches wider at the top than at the bottom.

**template** — a full-size pattern of wood or metal used for repetitive layout.

**temporary brace** — 1" x 6" board, 8 to 16 feet long, used to stabilize members of the frame during raising.

**temporary post** — a timber with square-cut ends used to support some timbers during the raising process, or until masonry is built.

**tensile force** — forces of tension.

**thickness** — the smaller dimension of a given timber.

**timber frame** — a load-carrying structure of timbers ranging in size from 4" x 4"s to 9" x 15"s.

**timber hand saw** — five or six point hand saw with the teeth set for cross-cut sawing.

**tongue** — the shorter blade of a framing square that is 16 inches long and 1½ inches wide.

**tongue and groove** — a term describing boards which fit together, edge to edge; one board has a projection and the other has a slot.

**transit** — a telescope mounted at a right angle to a horizontal axis; includes its own level; used for siting straight lines.

**transitional force** — a force passing from one place to another.

**trenail** — an oak dowel used for securing joints approximately 2 inches in diameter.

**trimming out** — framing around or otherwise strengthening an opening through a floor, roof, or wall.

**true scarf joint** — another term for a simple scarf joint (see diagram).

**tusk joint** — a mortise and tenon joint in which the tenon goes all the way through the corresponding mortise.

**waste** — the portion of wood cut away to reveal the joint.

**wattle and daub** — woven sticks smeared with mud used to fill in the open areas of the timber frame on the exterior walls, generally covered with clapboards, and plaster inside.

**weather-tight** — a structure which is covered with siding and a roof, and which has windows and doors, so that the inside stays dry.

**wedge** — a piece of metal tapering to a thin edge; used for splitting wood.

**width** — the larger dimension of a given timber.

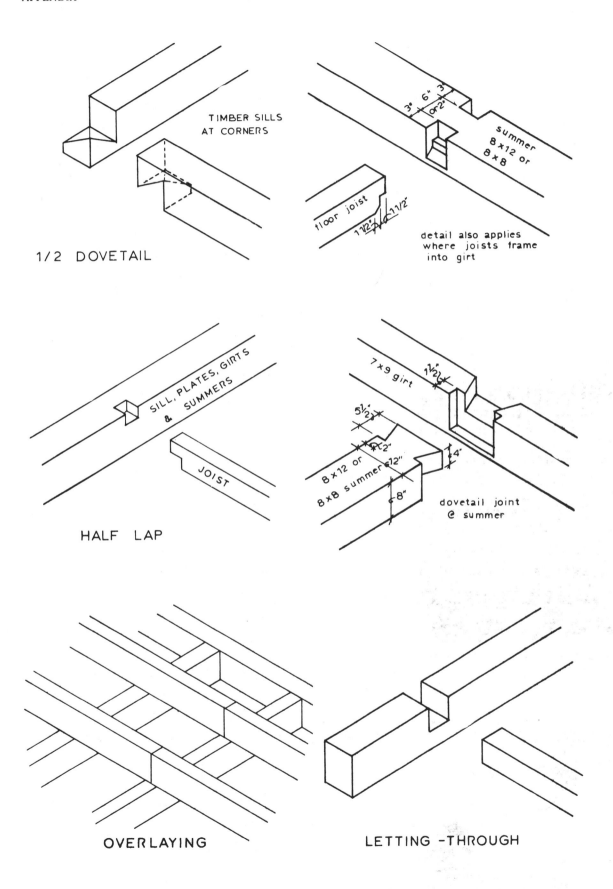

1/2  DOVETAIL

TIMBER SILLS
AT CORNERS

floor joist

summer
8 x 12 or
8 x 8

detail also applies
where joists frame
into girt

HALF  LAP

SILL, PLATES, GIRTS
& SUMMERS

JOIST

7 x 9 girt

8 x 12 or
8 x 8 summer

dovetail joint
@ summer

OVERLAYING                        LETTING -THROUGH

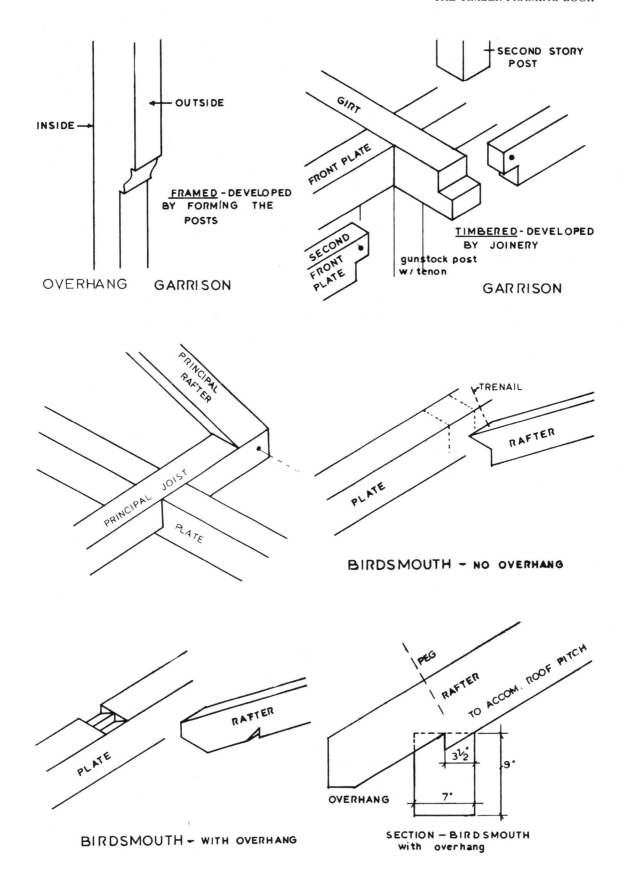

INSIDE →                    ← OUTSIDE

FRAMED - DEVELOPED
BY FORMING THE
POSTS

OVERHANG    GARRISON

SECOND STORY
POST

GIRT

FRONT PLATE

SECOND
FRONT
PLATE

TIMBERED - DEVELOPED
BY JOINERY

gunstock post
w/ tenon

GARRISON

PRINCIPAL
RAFTER

PRINCIPAL JOIST

PLATE

TRENAIL

RAFTER

PLATE

BIRDSMOUTH - NO OVERHANG

PLATE

RAFTER

BIRDSMOUTH - WITH OVERHANG

PEG

RAFTER

TO ACCOM. ROOF PITCH

3½"

9"

OVERHANG

7"

SECTION - BIRDSMOUTH
with overhang

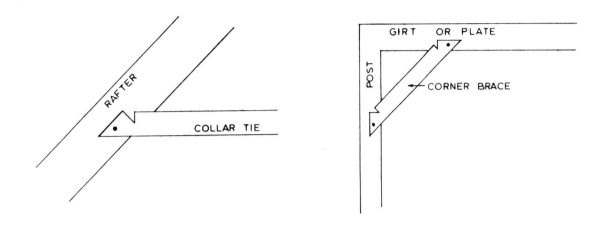

1/2   DOVETAIL

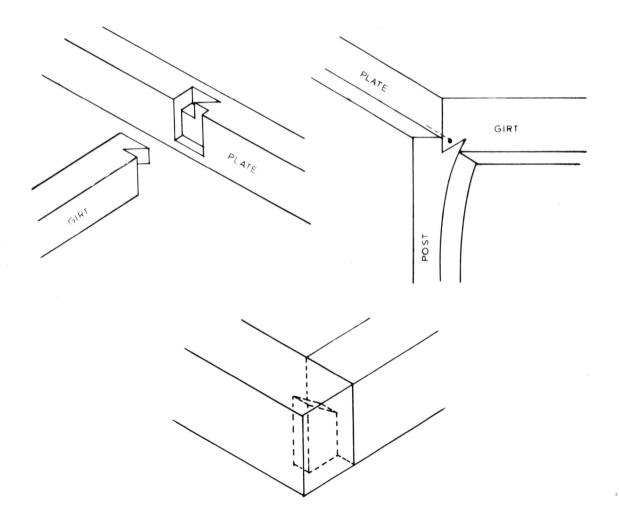

## MODIFIED MORTISE & TENON AT RAFTER PEAK

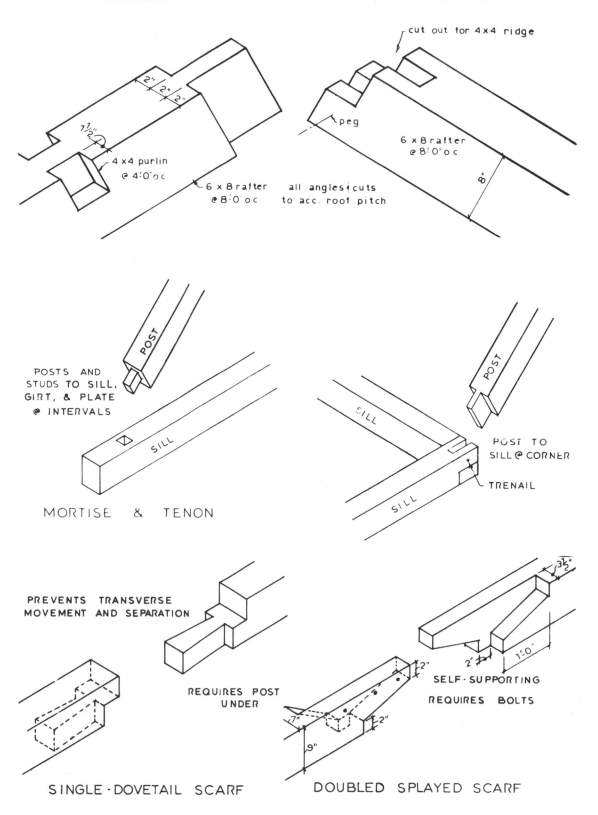

cut out for 4x4 ridge

2"   2"   2"

1 1/2"

4x4 purlin
@ 4'-0" o.c.

6 x 8 rafter
@ 8'-0" o.c.       all angles cuts
to acc. roof pitch

peg

6 x 8 rafter
@ 8'-0" o.c.

8"

POSTS AND
STUDS TO SILL,
GIRT, & PLATE
@ INTERVALS

POST

SILL

MORTISE & TENON

SILL

POST

POST TO
SILL @ CORNER

TRENAIL

SILL

PREVENTS TRANSVERSE
MOVEMENT AND SEPARATION

REQUIRES POST
UNDER

SINGLE-DOVETAIL SCARF

3 1/2"

2"

1'-0"

SELF-SUPPORTING

REQUIRES BOLTS

2"

7"

2"

9"

DOUBLED SPLAYED SCARF

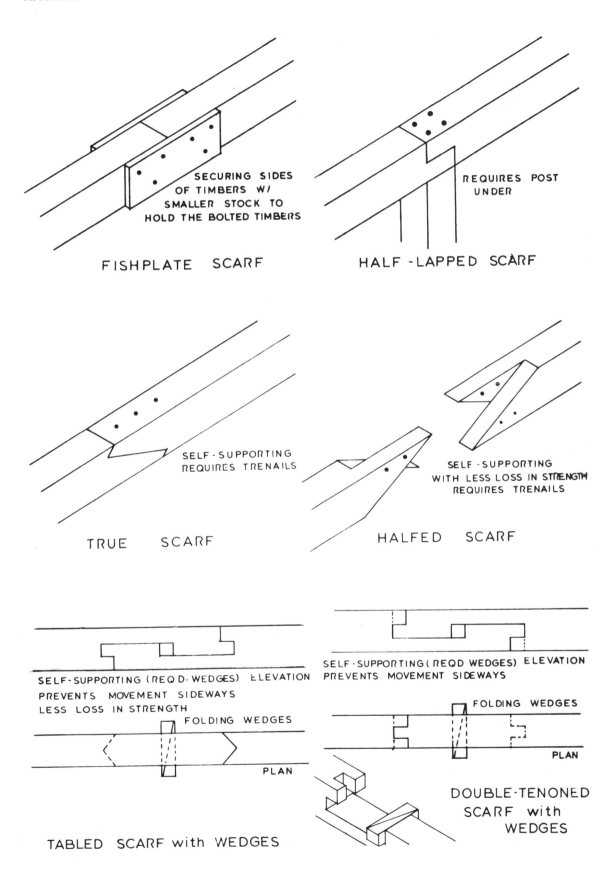

FISHPLATE SCARF

SECURING SIDES
OF TIMBERS w/
SMALLER STOCK TO
HOLD THE BOLTED TIMBERS

HALF-LAPPED SCARF

REQUIRES POST
UNDER

TRUE SCARF

SELF-SUPPORTING
REQUIRES TRENAILS

HALFED SCARF

SELF-SUPPORTING
WITH LESS LOSS IN STRENGTH
REQUIRES TRENAILS

TABLED SCARF with WEDGES

SELF-SUPPORTING (REQD. WEDGES) ELEVATION
PREVENTS MOVEMENT SIDEWAYS
LESS LOSS IN STRENGTH

FOLDING WEDGES

PLAN

DOUBLE-TENONED
SCARF with
WEDGES

SELF-SUPPORTING (REQD WEDGES) ELEVATION
PREVENTS MOVEMENT SIDEWAYS

FOLDING WEDGES

PLAN

—